IN SEARCH
of the
CROSS

Learning to "Glory" In It

Robert J. Wieland

GLAD TIDINGS PUBLISHERS
8784 Valley View Drive
Berrien Springs, MI 49103 USA

In Search of the Cross ⌐ *Learning to "Glory" In It*
Robert J. Wieland
Copyright © 1999 by
Glad Tidings Publishers

Book and cover design by Nova Artworks

PRINTED IN U.S.A.

ISBN 0-9635077-5-3

Dedication

~

DEDICATED to my African friends in Uganda and Kenya,
who patiently (and sometimes eagerly) listened
to these ideas in Luganda and Swahili

Preface

When I lived in Florida I used to go swimming in the Atlantic Ocean. There I soon learned something about the force of the undertow that can sweep a strong person off his feet. All one's paddling and flailing of arms and legs is useless to resist the power of a riptide.

Every one of us knows firsthand the force of the undertow of temptation that pulls the strongest man or woman into the tide of sin. We *try* to stand, but around us swirls this overmastering force.

The source of this undertow of temptation is what the Bible calls the "world." Try your hardest to be "good," and there is the "world" twenty-four hours a day trying its best to sweep you off your feet with its tide of temptation.

What to do? Is there any way to neutralize this undertow, any way *always* to conquer temptation?

The New Testament says there is. But the "way" is not too well known. It was Paul who wrote, "I will boast only about the cross of our Lord Jesus Christ; for by means of His cross *the world is dead to me,* and I am dead to the world." Galatians 6:14, TEV. "God forbid that I should glory except in the cross of our Lord Jesus Christ, by whom the world has been crucified to me, and I to the world," NKJV.

That's a pretty high claim! What he calls "the cross" is a truth that cancels out the power of the undertow that sweeps us into sin. When you and I learn to "glory in the cross" only, we too will stand secure and solid; and the fiercest temptations Satan can possibly invent will be powerless to sweep us away.

So many thoughtlessly say, "It's hard to follow Christ, and it's easy to be lost." The truth is that once we see the powerful truth that is in the message of the cross, *it's easy to follow Christ, and it's hard to be lost.* The "undertow" is "dead." Jesus stood firm as a rock as temptation beat upon Him; we can stand with Him.

Do you want to find out why? May this book give you a clearer understanding of the power of the message of the cross. Take a good look; it will change your life.

Contents

Chapter 1

WHY SEARCH FOR THE CROSS?

⟋⟍

IF YOU HAVE A NEW ROLLS-ROYCE, YOU WANT TO KEEP IT POLISHED LIKE NEW. You may not say a word, but you are proud of your possession. Your incessant polishing says you "glory" in it.

Others show off fine clothes, a house or ranch, or revel in a brilliant career. Their music, art, science, or other hobbies and achievements are all they can talk about.

The apostle Paul had an obsession, which is the subject of this book. According to one version, he says, "God forbid that I should glory except in the cross of our Lord Jesus Christ." Galatians 6:14.

That strange word "glory" eludes us, for we have no word in modern English that fully covers what it means. Combine all the will to attain, the pride of possession, the passion to know and appreciate, the charm of beauty, the yearning for thrills that we moderns know in our endless quest for life's pleasures, then you can begin to sense what Paul meant when he said, "I ... glory ... in the cross." "I determined not to know anything among you except Jesus Christ and Him crucified." 1 Corinthians 2:2.

WAS THIS MAN A FANATIC?

What did he see in the cross of Christ that inspired in him a life-long passion such as Michael Jordan had for basketball, Picasso for painting, or Yo Yo Ma for Bach? Is there something vital and compelling in the Bible that we are missing?

Scientists tell us that there are vast untapped resources of energy in ocean water, enough to meet mankind's needs for power for generations to come. There are also vast untapped resources of spiritual energy in the cross that Paul tells us about so enthusiastically. Most of us make our faith into a toilsome and agonizing ordeal. We are simply ignorant of the gospel's largely untapped capacity for changing people— a power that Paul plugged into.

His very conversion came as the result of a vision of Christ as the *crucified* One. He had been deeply immersed in hateful prejudice, but in one brief hour he saw that the cross where Jesus died proved His claims to be the long-awaited Messiah. That flash of insight on his way to Damascus invested the cross with an irresistible charm that never dimmed for him. Henceforth the cross was the sun shining in his sky, the gem itself of gospel truth—not a mere facet of it. It was the center and heart of Paul's message from then on.

Our modern world knows little or nothing about that cross. To the ancient world it was a focal point of attention, "foolishness" to many, or a "stumbling block," and always an "offense." 1 Corinthians 1:23; Galatians 5:11. But to the world today it is blah, a boring puzzle. "The offense of the cross" has not ceased, but the cross cannot be an offense if it is not understood.

It's no wonder that the world today is apathetic. Rather than fighting it as Paul's world did, the modem world is steeped in lifeless ignorance of it. Yet one sees crosses almost everywhere—on churches, around people's necks, in stained glass windows. Why such ignorance of its meaning?

How Satan shot himself in the foot.

This darkness has been brought about by the cunning plans of the enemy of all good. Satan knew that the cross assured his utter defeat and exposed his complete depravity. It rang his death knell. All the universe of God watched Jesus die, like spectators in the grandstands watching a fight in the arena. Satan's hatred of Christ displayed in the crucifixion uprooted him forever from any tiny root of sympathy or affection in that vast audience. In this sense "the ruler of this world" was "cast out" when Jesus died on His cross. See John 12:31-33.

His mask torn off once and for all, Satan retained no sympathy from heavenly angels. No one who knew God's true character ever again would waste a thought of pity on Satan. So far as the great hosts of unfallen angels were concerned, Satan knew he had lost his case. All he could do now would be to hope to get this newly created planet on his side, and with that advantage wage "war" against Christ.

THERE REALLY IS A BEHIND-THE-SCENES CONSPIRACY!

Thus he formed his malignant design to blot the knowledge of the cross from the understanding of mankind. In setting up the "abomination of desolation" (Daniel 12:11), he forged a counterfeit of true Christianity. Its basic principle was to make a detour around the cross so that mankind should not get so much as a glimpse of its *meaning*. To fasten us in his deception, Satan was to exalt *the sign of the cross* to be worshipped, to the exclusion of *the truth of the cross*.

Thus from the days of Constantine the sign of the cross became the emblem of professed Christianity, while a subtle counterfeit of the gospel wrought a "transgression of desolation" in the human heart. See Daniel 8:11-13. Christendom's history for over 1,600 years offers a pathetic comment on Satan's "great wrath" against the gospel, "because he knows that he has a short time." Revelation 12:12. He has offered men a shadow in place of the substance. Those crosses worn about the neck or erected on church steeples or glazed in church windows are a familiar talisman, a charm or amulet, an adornment. Crosses of wood or metal are even worshipped, while the genuine, the *principle* of the cross, is unknown.

So confident is Satan of his plans that he freely permits talking about the cross, praying about it, singing about it, wearing it, using it as an architectural emblem, even worshipping it, just so long as he can thwart any attempt toward *understanding what happened there.* What more clever trick can a defeated enemy perfect than to take the sign of his defeat and transform it into an emblem of his victory?

The sun has truly been blotted from the sky of such "Christianity." Although the truth of the cross may not be consciously disbelieved or rejected, yet the failure to grasp its meaning results in a tragic loss, just as much as the rejection of the cross meant to the Jewish leaders of Christ's day. The mind accepts the symbol while the heart fails to realize the experience.

THE GREATEST CONSPIRACY DEFEAT OF ALL HISTORY.

But we need not be misled by the meaningless symbol of an empty word. The forging of the counterfeit was meant only to forestall a search for the genuine. But the very existence of the counterfeit suggests that somewhere we shall find the genuine! The clouds and mist that Satan has sought to throw about the cross will be lifted for us, and we will come to see in breathtaking reality the same glorious revelation that Paul saw. What Satan hoped would be his *coup d'état* turned out for him to be a self-inflicted total defeat.

Our personal victory over Satan is assured in these words: "They overcame him by the blood of the Lamb." Revelation 12:11. When and where was that blood shed? At the cross. John the Baptist's words still make sense: "*Behold!* The Lamb of God who takes away the sin of the world." John 1:29. "*Look* to Me, and be saved," is what God asks us to do. Isaiah 45:22.

LOOKING IS PEOPLE'S FAVORITE PASTIME.

News magazines capitalize on this desire to "look" at something new. Millions spend their idle hours just watching the parade of humanity passing by their doors or their TV screens, or poring through picture magazines. If there is an accident on the freeway or anything unusual, we have an urge to "behold." All have this built-in yearning to feast our eyes on some sight *yet unseen.* There is an unsatisfied longing to see something ultimate.

> Upon that cross of Jesus my eye at times can see
> The very dying form of One who suffered there for me.
> And from my smitten heart, with tears two wonders I confess:
> The wonders of redeeming love, and my unworthiness.
>
> I take O cross your shadow for my abiding place!
> I ask no other sunshine, than the sunshine of His face.
> Content to let the world go by, to know no gain nor loss
> My sinful self my only shame, my glory all the cross.
> ⤷ Elizabeth Clephane

What we long to see is that cross of Jesus. No other sight can satisfy.

And once we have seen it, like Paul, we will "glory" in nothing else. It will become our passion. If we "behold the Lamb of God," we will see a sight that has power to dissolve all idolatry into the nothingness that it is. Money, possessions, careers, fame, sensual pleasure, all lose their charm for the person who has *seen* what Calvary means. Life begins.

Let us look.

Chapter 2

THE CROSS AS NATURE'S MYSTERY

ᨠ

NATURE HASN'T WANTED TO HIDE ITS SECRET. But for thousands of years sinful man trod the soil of this planet without seeing the most simple and elemental secret written there—the way of the cross.

The farmer cast seed into the ground to produce his daily food without realizing the lesson each seed would teach him: that fruitful life comes only through surrender of life to death, so a new creature can come forth.

When at last a sinless Youth trod our soil, day after day He knelt upon it to pray to His Father for strength and wisdom to bring to man the answers to our questions: How can the problem of death be solved? How can the human race be redeemed from extinction? How can bad people become good?

HIS AMAZING DISCOVERY.

As Creator, Jesus had written the book of nature with His own hands. Now, as a Man, He sought to understand it, to draw from its mysteries a lesson that would point others to the only way of life—the way of the cross.

Later, when visitors from Greece asked to see Jesus, He answered them, "The hour has come that the Son of man should be glorified.... Unless a grain of wheat falls into the ground and dies, it remains alone; but if it dies, it produces much grain. He who loves his life will lose it;

and be who hates his life in this world will keep it for eternal life." "'I, if I am lifted up from the earth, will draw all peoples to Myself.' This He said, signifying by what death He would die." John 12:23-25, 32, 33.

The seed that seeks "security" laid up in a vessel on a shelf comes to nothing because in cherishing its precious "self" it "remains alone." Though without fault, only that seed conquers death that finds a lonely grave within the darkened earth. Only by dying can it bring forth "much fruit" (KJV).

A TINY SEED TEACHES A POWERFUL LESSON!

To the sinless Youth seeking to discern the mystery, each flowering petal, each towering forest tree, bespoke a Gethsemane-like sacrifice for some little seed that died alone in the earth. What glory out of all proportion to its sacrifice does the tiny grape seed attain in the heavy vines laden with purple clusters of fruit! So, the Son of God knew, would His sacrifice become the means of "bringing many sons to glory." Hebrews 2:10.

Through His young soul surged a mighty commitment: He would count Himself a "seed," and cast His security and all that was precious to Him forever into the "soil" to die. Thus He drew from nature the elemental principle, previously undiscerned, that led to His wondrous cross, the secret weapon that vanquishes death.

It doesn't matter whether Jesus as a boy fully understood that His sacrificial death would assume the form of a Roman crucifixion. What is important is that this ancient criminal death, the most shameful and spectacular, was the best way for the whole world to "see" the demonstration of His sacrificial love. For Him, to "fall into the ground and die" as a "seed" was more painful and bitter than enduring a mere physical death. The apostle Paul suggests a great contrast between "the death on the cross" and ordinary death. See Philippians 2:8. The full measure of ultimate death, the real thing that is infinitely more than the "sleep" we think of as death, is despair and shame to the uttermost. Jesus' cross embraced that full measure.

But today the cross means little to us, because history has secured an almost complete reversal of values. Once suggesting the most ignominious and degrading torture a human being could endure, a death almost too terrible for even a demon to merit, the cross is now the world's most honored emblem.

The reason for such a transformation in value lies deeper than a mere fortune of history. No hero worship centered in a martyr's death could secure the awesome appreciation multitudes of intelligent people feel for Christ's cross. To discover the reason for this appreciation is the purpose of this book.

THE CROSS TOUCHES THE TENDER NERVE OF OUR DEEPEST, INMOST NEED.

Whether or not we profess to be religious, we need only a glimpse of its significance in order to be aware that there is something within the depths of our being which responds. The truth of the cross awakens strange overtones of appreciation, chords within human nature that nothing else can touch. History points to its own climax and objective when this truth shall at last penetrate the awakened conscience of every human being on earth.

Every one knows that a tender tie binds his soul to Calvary because the One who died there is so close to him as to be almost himself. There can be no sympathy with anyone else on earth so close as His sympathy with us and our sympathy with Him while He hangs on His cross. Since Christ died for all, "they all share in His death." 2 Corinthians 5:14, TEV. The truth-seeker knows this, and the truth-evader cannot avoid a confrontation with the truth he or she seeks to reject.

Believer or unbeliever, every one will likewise ultimately know the *power* revealed at the cross. "I, if I be lifted up from the earth, will draw *all peoples* to Myself," says the Crucified One. We may choose to resist this "drawing" felt within our souls, but before any of us can possibly suffer the pain of being lost, we will be obliged persistently to resist. Rejecting love, "all those who hate Me love death," Christ says. Proverbs 8:36.

BUT IF WE CHOOSE NOT TO RESIST, WE ARE "DRAWN" TO CHRIST THROUGH HIS CROSS.

A million devils, opposing through all the circumstances of life, are as powerless to counteract this drawing as is a thread to restrain a surging battleship. Jesus' words to the inquiring Greeks can be understood only as a claim to universal power over the hearts of all people through the uplifting of His cross. No, it is not a claim that all will be saved, but that all will feel in some measure the drawing power of the cross, some to yield, and others perversely to resist.

THERE IS AN ALMOST IRRESISTIBLE CHARM IN CHRIST'S CROSS.

What is it? Something invests Christ's cross with an appeal to the one who pauses to contemplate its meaning. If its Victim were merely a fanatical zealot or deranged mystic with a pitiable delusion that He was divine, or if He were merely a good man tragically murdered, His death would make no more lasting impression on recurring generations than a martyr dying or the assassination of a statesman. Mankind would soon forget. *The Victim's claim to be God is what accounts for the timeless appeal of His death.*

But how can we know that He is divine? Is our faith rooted merely in tradition or superstition? Is our desire for eternal reward so strong that we are willing to assume the incredible in order to escape from the hard world in which we live?

A glimpse of the cross is better than all the labored arguments employed to prove that Jesus is divine. Once discern the nature of the love (*agape*) revealed there, and the Victim stands out clearly as none other than the Son of God. Only "God is love [*agape*]" 1 John 4:8. Human love alone could never stage or invent the demonstration we see there. The quality of love revealed is self-emptying, infinitely beyond our calculating, self-centered human love which easily fails test. Every one's heart convicts him that such *agape* must come from God alone, and that the hostility which murdered the Victim there was in essence our own "enmity against God." Romans 8:7. Jesus' *agape* carries its own built-in witness to prove its credentials are divine. That love was unearthly. No philosopher, poet, playwright, in thousands of years had dreamed of such a love.

This love sends the appeal of the cross home to human hearts in the awareness that the One who died thereon is every person's truest and closest relative, the unfailing Friend or Elder Brother who has always loved us when we were most inclined to hate ourselves, the Companion who has remained with us in our shadows and believed in us when we doubted and disowned ourselves.

Every person has at times been faintly conscious of this brightest of all hopes—that Someone trusted him and believed in him while knowing the fullness of all his guilty secrets. Sweeter than the words "I love you" is the assurance, "I believe in you; I trust you all the way; I risk everything on your future."

No MERELY HUMAN VOICE COULD SPEAK SUCH ASSURANCE TO US!

Since we know our sins are infinite, only an infinite forgiveness and trust could so encourage us. That every one has heard this Voice of hope and encouragement is evidence to us all that the Son of God has come in our "flesh." We may resist and drown the Voice, but if we listen to it, we will be impelled to follow Him.

The Voice that speaks to our hearts and the truth written in nature—both disclose the heavenly origin of the principle of the cross.

This little book makes no pretense of reaching beyond a *search* for the cross. When we conclude our visit together, the search will have only begun for us both. The vast reservoir of truth yet unrealized is a pledge that there must be an endless life to come that will be devoted to a quest for the meaning of that infinite sacrifice. Our search will grow into the science and song of the redeemed throughout eternity.

Chapter 3

JESUS' FIRST LESSON ON THE MEANING OF THE CROSS

⌒

WHY DID HE POSTPONE THE LESSON SO LONG? It is surprising to discover that Jesus waited until nearly the close of His three years of ministry before He clearly told the disciples about His crucifixion to come.

When we remember that the teaching of the cross is the one central theme of the gospel, the sun in the firmament of heavenly truth, we wonder why the Savior so long delayed instruction on that all-important subject.

Only an occasional mystic reference had He made to His death. There were only His remarks about "this temple" being destroyed and raised again in three days (John 2:19), of His being lifted up as the bronze serpent (John 3:14), of giving His "flesh" for the life of the world (John 6:51), of the sign of the prophet Jonah (Matthew 12:39), or of a sad separation of the Bridegroom from "the children of the bridechamber" (Matthew 9:15, KJV).

But the disciples did not catch the meaning of these pregnant utterances. What they needed was a clear, full story of the soul-shaking event to come. This Jesus did not divulge until His visit to the coasts of Caesarea Philippi only a few months before the great trial of faith itself took place.

It is also surprising that not until the same time did Jesus venture to ask the disciples who they thought He really was. Time must be allowed them to nurture the first superficial enthusiasm roused by His early ministry into the more sober conviction of a faith that could endure trial.

AND INDEED THEIR FAITH IN JESUS' DEITY *WAS* SORELY TRIED.

Reticent to take to Himself the title "Son of God," He found a strange pleasure in persistently calling Himself the "Son of man." He had progressively disappointed the fond hopes of the Jews regarding their expected Messiah. Steadfastly declining the applause of people who would like to see in Him the fulfillment of their popular hopes, He seemed all too content to remain in poverty and obscurity. He took no interest in courting the approval of the religious "establishment," but instead pursued a course that appeared needlessly to attract their enmity.

After the difficult discourse on the Bread of Life (John 6), multitudes of former disciples went back to walk no more with Him. He even dared abruptly to dismiss a crowd who purposed to make Him king. Now He was becoming "despised and rejected of men." The disciples could find every excuse, it seemed, to renounce even a purely human, worldly faith in Jesus as the Christ.

HOW THE DISCIPLES FINALLY RECOGNIZED CHRIST.

At the same time they had seen plenty of evidence to confirm the insistent convictions of the Holy Spirit that this Man was indeed the Messiah, the Son of God. And this evidence was not merely the physical miracles He performed. These could be explained away by friend or foe, or at least disregarded. Physical miracles seldom strengthen true faith. What *did* confirm the faith of the disciples was the unworldly, supernatural, truly miraculous love seen in every word and act of Jesus. There was profound spiritual wisdom and heavenly common sense in all He said. These were the "very works" for whose sake Jesus appealed to Philip to believe Him. John 14:11, 12, KJV. Refusal to recognize *these* "works" was the hopeless and incurable sin of unbelief on the part of the Jewish leaders, not against the Son of man, but against the Holy Spirit.

But the disciples believed! Now at Caesarea Philippi, within a few months of the crucifixion, they were at last ready to confess their faith.

"When Jesus came into the region of Caesarea Philippi, He asked His disciples, saying, 'Who do men say that I, the Son of Man, am?'" Matthew 16:13. Their replies would have been flattering to anyone— except the Son of God. Popular fancy acclaimed Him as Elijah, Jeremiah, or another of the prophets. Unsatisfied, Jesus proceeded to ask His disciples to crystallize their somewhat vague conceptions into a confession of deep conviction. He put them on the spot: "But who do you say that I am?" Verse 15.

Peter was the first to find words to express the bold faith that had gripped their souls. Not only was this Man a greater than all the prophets; not only was He the long-expected human Messiah. "You are the Christ, the Son of the living God," he boldly confessed. Verse 16.

Jesus commended Peter's faith, but quickly cautioned him against the sin of supposing he deserved credit for it: "Blessed are you, Simon Bar-Jonah, for flesh and blood has not revealed this to you, but My Father who is in heaven." Verse 17. Peter must not be self-sufficient as though he were more clever than others.

As brilliant as fleshly brain cells may be, unless aided by the Holy Spirit the human mind is utterly incapable of recognizing God when He appears incognito. "No one can say that Jesus is Lord except by the Holy Spirit." 1 Corinthians 12:3. The Son of God walked the dusty thoroughfares of life two thousand years ago quite unperceived and unrecognized by humanity, even as in all the years since then heavenly truth has been equally unperceived by "flesh and blood."

NOW JESUS GOES TO WORK TO TELL THE FULL TRUTH.

With the disciples' confession of faith, Jesus was now ready to lay the foundation and cornerstone of His church. "On this rock [that is, this confession of My identity] I will build My church, and the gates of Hades shall not prevail against it." Matthew 16:18. We now see Him laboring swiftly, skillfully, a wise Master Builder and divine Craftsman, erecting an edifice of faith against which "the gates of hell" shall not prevail.

Now that the disciples were thoroughly convinced of His divinity, He was prepared to enlighten them about His death. Drawing aside all the mystic veils that had beclouded the previous brief references to the cross, He plainly, even bluntly, told them that He must be rejected and slain: "From that time Jesus began to show to His disciples that He must go to Jerusalem, and suffer many things from the elders and chief priests and scribes, and be killed, and be raised again the third day." Verse 21.

BAD NEWS!

The disciples listened with more astonishment than terror. The idea of God having a Son was revolutionary enough to their Jewish minds; now the thought of that Son of God *dying* seemed incredulous. This cannot be! A crucified Messiah in place of a glorified, crowned, world-ruling one? This was an insult to their intelligence, a scandal and a reproach. The more convinced the disciples were that Jesus was the Son of God, the more confused and confounded they were to be told that He must be put to death. And by the best people in the world, their own nation!

Now the same "blessed" Simon Bar-Jonah who had been first to confess the Son of God was first to deny His cross. Solicitous, apparently, even for Jesus' mental health at hearing the astounding announcement so repugnant to his colleagues, the well-meaning Peter rudely grasped the person of his Lord as if to give Him a kind of shock treatment to jar Him from such morbid imaginings. No ill treatment could be accorded *Him* by members of the human race, especially by the Chosen People! "Then Peter took Him aside, and began to rebuke Him, saying, 'Far be it from You, Lord; this shall not happen to You.'" Verse 22. Crosses are for felons, not for anyone good, and especially not for One who is the Son of God!

Thus was the cross both a "stumbling block" and "foolishness" to the first disciples, and an "offense" as well. Thus is it even today to our human nature.

WE NEED NOT BE SURPRISED AT THE CONFUSION OF THE DISCIPLES.

If "flesh and blood" could not comprehend the idea that Jesus was the Son of God, much less could Peter unaided comprehend the doctrine of the cross. The very idea was something so utterly beyond human invention as to be unfathomable to their minds without the revelation of the Holy Spirit.

It was good that Jesus had first drawn from the disciples their confession that He was the Son of God before springing this shocking news on them. Otherwise they would have bolted in unbelief and abandoned Him as did so many others of His interested followers had just done. Man-made religions could invent "messiahs," but none could conceive of a suffering, dying Messiah giving Himself in unutterable love for the world.

ARE WE BETTER OR WISER THAN PETER?

Our unaided human thinking today is just as blind to the truth of the cross as was that of the first disciples. We are in even greater peril; we have what they did not have—a mental knowledge of the facts of the crucifixion and a nearly universal recognition that it really happened, but this "head knowledge" can confuse the avenues of approach to a heart understanding of the cross.

If we have the least idea that our fortunate birth in the Christian era now gives us any advantage over Peter, we may feel that we naturally are wiser than he was, living as we do in a more enlightened age. We have graduated out of spiritual ignorance like his! And then, we miss the whole point of the gospel.

We cannot even begin to comprehend what took place at Caesarea Philippi unless we realize that our human nature is the same as was

Peter's. Failure to recognize this may expose us to the tragedy of repeating on a fatal plane Peter's spurning of the cross. He spurned it ignorantly; we may be in danger of rejecting it knowingly. Incidentally, *that* will be the final sin of lost people.

THE REASON WHY PETER REACTED AS HE DID IS OBVIOUS.

The idea of the cross was something so original, unworldly, that it could arise only in the mind of God. The cross is both the "wisdom" and the "power" of God. 1 Corinthians 1:18, 24. It is a divine strategy of spiritual warfare of sublime skill. But Peter's response to the Savior's stunning announcement was the same as that which people of every place and age would experience. He was expressing the thoughts of our own hearts, even today, in treating as repugnant foolishness the very idea of being crucified.

Jesus revealed this insight in His rebuke to Peter for his disrespect-ful and irreverent interruption: "You are an offense to Me, for you are not mindful of the things of God, but the things of men." Matthew 16:23. Peter was simply a man, as any one of us is, who could comprehend only the things that are of men! Peter was no more "wicked" than any of us—he was just being himself. And being himself, he couldn't fathom "the things of God" enough to discern the meaning of the cross. Those "things of men" which blinded his understanding blind ours as well.

But we have not yet considered the real source of Peter's opposition to our Lord's cross. Jesus was not rude or angry with the poor man, and His words were no passionate outburst of temper. The unmitigated severity of His stinging rebuke to His beloved disciple reveals a significant origin of Peter's worldly sentiments. Jesus was merely putting His finger of recognition on the plague spot of *mankind's* opposition to the cross: "He turned, and said to Peter, 'Get behind Me, Satan! You are an offense to Me.'" Verse 23.

Poor Peter!

He had unwittingly let himself be a tool in the hands of Satan by seeking to turn Jesus away from His sacrificial purpose. That temptation was real to Jesus! Christ saw that Peter's ideas had their source in the enemy's original rebellion in heaven. Evading His cross was an alluring temptation to Jesus that He had to resist with all the power of His will. Serving as Satan's amanuensis, Peter had touched a raw nerve in Jesus' soul.

We are not to understand that Peter was Satan himself, but Peter's attitude toward the cross was more than a reflection of fallible, uninformed human nature. It perfectly reflected the attitude of Satan himself.

We can imagine that the disciples by now were a subdued and quiet group as the full force of Jesus' pointed rebuke began to sink into their minds.

Chapter 4

HOW LUCIFER CHOSE TO HATE THE CROSS

⟿

F "FLESH AND BLOOD" COULD NOT COMPREHEND THE IDEA OF THE CROSS, COULD SATAN UNDERSTAND IT? There is nothing dense or unintelligent about him—he understands well what he is doing.

Therefore, in order to be the enemy of the cross, he must have understood it clearly. Were there a residual knowledge of salvation unknown to him, to that extent his opposition to truth would be blind and innocent. He could not then be "the devil and Satan." But knowing fully, Satan rebels.

Why must always remain the inscrutable "mystery of iniquity." The *how* of his rebellion included the most determined and intelligent scorning of the cross.

Peter in his human innocence was treading too near to the former Lucifer's ground when he tried to turn Jesus away from the cross.

When Satan tempted Adam and Eve in the Garden of Eden, his bait was the assurance that in transgression they would reach a higher life than they had been created to enjoy. "You will be as God," he promised. Genesis 3:5, Hebrew. This desire to be as God was the same that led to Satan's original sin in heaven:

"How you are fallen from heaven, O Lucifer, son
of the morning! How you are cut down to the ground,

you who weakened the nations! For you have said in your heart: '*I* will ascend into heaven, *I* will exalt my throne above the stars of God; *I* will also sit on the mount of the congregation on the farthest sides of the north; *I* will ascend above the heights of the clouds, *I* will be like the Most High.'" Isaiah 14:12-14.

No one can be *as* God without in fact seeking to *displace* God, because there can be only one "Most High."

LUCIFER'S LUST LED TO SELF-LOVE.

This has now become the natural "mind" of us all, apart from redemption. But the love of self leads to an "enmity against God." Romans 8:7. Enmity in turn leads to murder. Jesus said of the devil, "He was a murderer from the beginning." John 8:44. This is true because "whoever hates his brother is a murderer." 1 John 3:15. Satan hated God, and was jealous of Him. So in the very beginning of Lucifer's heavenly rebellion, the stark outline of a cross began to take shape in the shadows of eternity's history.

Doubtless Lucifer began to see where his rebellion would lead. He saw that the crime he nurtured in his soul was a dark and ugly one— that of murdering the eternal Son of God. So terrible is one's devotion to the love of self! Five times in Isaiah's passage we read of Lucifer's passion for his "I." Sin has its root in self-centeredness *indulged.*

Satan's root problem was a hatred of the idea of *agape,* a love which is God's character, totally different than anything we humans naturally think of as "love." Our kind of "love" loves nice people; *agape* loves bad, mean people. Our love is dependent on the beauty of its object; *agape* loves ugly people, even our enemies. Our love depends on the quality of its object; *agape* creates value in its object. Our love always wants to climb up higher just as Lucifer wanted to set his throne "above the stars of God;" *agape* is a love that dares to step down lower, as the Son of God did in those seven steps of amazing condescension listed in Philippians 2:5-8. Our human love always want to get; *agape* is always ready to give. Our human love seeks a reward; *agape* dares to relinquish it.

Last of all, what Satan hated the most was the ultimate revelation of *agape* displayed in Christ: *agape* dares to surrender eternal life, to die the second death. That is the supreme aspect of *agape* that Lucifer does not want the world or the universe to see. It's the opposite of everything he stands for.

Lucifer must have pondered long and earnestly the path he was choosing. Should he repent while there was still opportunity? If so, there could be only one way in which he might overcome the sin of his angelic soul—this wonderful "I" that sought to be "like the Most High" and to topple Him from His holy throne, would have to *die*. Self in Lucifer would have to be crucified.

HOW A BRIGHT ANGEL BECAME THE DEVIL, OR SATAN.

A spiritual cross on which Lucifer must die to self was the only way out of his dilemma in his incipient war with God. All his pride, his ego, his precious, darling "I" that he had cherished, must perish willingly of his own free choice so that only truth, and right, and holiness might live. Lucifer came so near to yielding that he was able to grasp the significance of the one way of deliverance for him.

Then emphatically, indignantly, irrevocably, he rejected the idea. No cross for him! Once for all, intelligently and responsibly, Lucifer repudiated the idea of self-denial and self-sacrifice. He would institute a new way of life for the vast universe of God—the love of the "I," the way of self-seeking, self-assertion, self-love. Thus Lucifer rejected the cross.

It was then that he became the devil and Satan, "that serpent of old, ... who deceives the whole world." Revelation 12:9. A bright angel who hates the cross becomes God's (and our) enemy.

This one bitter, unrelenting opponent to the divine principle of the cross well knows that the only avenue of return to righteousness for any sinful being in the universe is by way of the cross. Hence his studied, determined plan to blot the knowledge of that way from the consciousness of humanity. Anything satanic is anti-cross; the profound truth follows that anything anti-cross is satanic.

WHY WAS JESUS SO OUTSPOKEN TO PETER?

The Savior's stinging rebuke to him becomes more intelligible in this light. It was not an outburst of irritated temper on Jesus' part. Not only was Peter reflecting the "things of men," he was also reflecting the things of Satan! He was unwittingly voicing the sentiments of the enemy when he urged Jesus to put self-interest first and renounce the idea of going to Jerusalem to be crucified. Self-interest, self-concern, spiritual self-preservation, are uppermost thoughts to the soul of this fallen mighty angel. They now were to Peter, too. Are they not to us as well?

The "things of men" are shown to have an unfortunate spiritual origin, and Peter has revealed the problem to us. Peter found himself unconsciously in cooperation with Satan in his anti-cross campaign. Rightly understood, the temptation to turn Jesus aside from the cross was Satan's supreme weapon used over and over again throughout His earthly life.

Satan was not ignorant of the principle of the cross, but what he could not comprehend was the divine love revealed in the incarnate Christ that would lead Him to go all the way to the supreme sacrifice, and to do it voluntarily. The last malicious taunt flung at Christ was inspired by Satan—"Save Yourself, and come down from the cross!" Mark 15:30. And now at Caesarea Philippi self-interest is the ruling principle in the heart of dear Peter. He, too, is saying in effect, "Save Yourself, Lord." Jesus addressed him by his proper name when He said, "Get behind Me, Satan." Peter was anti-cross.

ARE WE LIKE PETER?

We would do well to refrain from a heart attitude of superiority over this man. He was a Christian, and he loved his Master ardently. Not only was he a "church member," he was an ordained minister as well. He could point with pride to the experience of actually casting out devils in the name of Christ! He had just been signally blessed by the commendation of Christ. And yet he was unconsciously in league with Satan in trying to oppose what Christ had to do!

We too are Christians who love our Lord ardently. We may work for Him, and we may point with pride and joy to an impressive lifework, rejoicing that apparently the devils are subject to us in Christ's name and that Satan falls like lightning from heaven at our mere word. Is it possible that we should unwittingly be in the same spiritual state of misunderstanding that Peter was in that day when our Lord said, "Get behind Me, Satan"?

If it was possible for dear, winsome, lovable Peter to be blindly in accord with the sentiments of the enemy, it may be no less so for us. Whether or not that highly undesirable epithet applies to us depends upon our heart attitude toward the cross.

"Let him that thinks he stands take heed lest he fall." With the disciples, we need to gather closely about Jesus to hear His next lesson on the meaning of the cross.

Chapter 5

JESUS' SECOND LESSON ON THE MEANING OF THE CROSS

ᗢ

P ETER WOULD BE SHOCKED WHEN HE HAD TIME TO CONSIDER WHAT HE HAD DONE. He had actually dared to rebuke his Master, and had even laid hands on Him as on a fellow fisherman that he thought was out of his mind.

An awed and deeply impressed group listened as Jesus for the first time clearly unfolded the law of the kingdom of heaven. Here is the real point of what it means to follow Him:

> "Then Jesus said to His disciples, 'If any one desires to come after Me, let him deny himself, and take up his cross, and follow Me. For whoever desires to save his life will lose it, but whoever loses his life for My sake will find it.'" Matthew 16:24, 25.

It was as if He said, in effect: You are astonished that I, the Son of God, must go to My cross and die. Not only so, but you yourselves, if you will follow Me, must each one surrender to die upon his cross with Me. We are in this together, and the law of the cross is binding upon us all!

THAT "WHOEVER" IS ALL-INCLUSIVE.
Neither God is excepted, nor man. In the distant ages of eternity

before sin began, Father and Son clasped hands in a solemn agreement that if man should sin, the Father was to give His Son, and the Son was to give Himself, that the universe might be saved from the ruin of self-seeking.

Further, in the end God would share His throne with all who would choose to share Christ's cross. For Him there must be a risking of everything in a dramatic expression of love, revealing depths and heights as yet undreamed of by sinless beings. God has *His* cross!

Whoever you are, if you follow Jesus, you have *your* cross. You need not be a priest, a monk, a clergyman, a missionary, or even a church officer or religious leader, in order to be included in the "whoever" who otherwise must lose his "life." The seed that would save its life will lose it; the seed that will die in the ground alone will bear much "fruit." Here, says Jesus, is the genius of principle on which My kingdom is founded.

It is no surprise that when sin challenged the government of God, it zeroed in to attack this principle of self-surrender at the cross. In the war that followed, divine love could find no other way to conquer than the way of the cross. Love chose it instinctively because it is its perfect expression. No other course could the Son of God have taken than to surrender to the cross.

Whenever genuine love (*agape*) meets the problem of sin, a cross is erected on which self is crucified. No other decision could the Father have made than to give His only-begotten Son, because He "so loved the world." In those dimly understood ages of eternity, the solemn agreement was entered into by the eternally preexistent Christ that He should become the Lamb of God. Because His heart was the infinite reservoir of love itself, He chose that way. Thus He was "slain from the foundation of the world." Revelation 13:8.

In whatever heart it enters today, divine love chooses alike when it meets the problem of sin. The principle of victory is the same whether it is the Creator wrestling with the problem, or you and I.

HOW THE BOY JESUS DISCOVERED THE CROSS.

The truth of the cross is beautifully illustrated in the experience of Jesus when He came to earth. Although He was fully man, "in all points tempted like as we are," yet His heart was without sin, and therefore pure. It thus remained—wonder of wonders!—the reservoir of love (*agape*). In that respect He differed from all other human beings who have been born into the world. He alone knew no sin, no *surrender* to egoism in any form although the temptation to self-indulgence was as real for Him as for us.

Yet we cannot suppose that any conscious memory of His preexistence remained with Him in His earthly childhood. As a babe in His mother's arms in the stable at Bethlehem, He had no conscious intelligence beyond that of other human babies at birth. He could not acknowledge the adoration of the shepherds or the wise men from the East. As a child in Nazareth, did He entertain Joseph and Mary with tales of the glories of heaven which He knew in His preexistence there? Like a fortunate child who has been to the "big city," did He tell his playmates in the rustic mountain village of His exploits as the Commander of the heavenly angels?

No; as a child, Jesus learned wisdom as we must learn. "The Child grew" and "increased in wisdom and stature." Luke 2:40, 52. The wonder of Christ is the wonder of His birth, God in human flesh, subject to the laws of mental and physical growth as we are all subject to them, yet "without sin." Certainly He was not born with any miraculous memory of His divine preexistence. All these divine advantages He laid aside.

THE IMPORTANCE OF THE AGE OF TWELVE.

By the time a child reaches that age, very deep thoughts can course through his/her mind. Patterns of choice are being formed that determine the whole of afterlife.

Jesus was twelve when He first visited the national festival of His people known as the Passover. For the first time He looked upon the famed temple and watched the white-robed priests lay a bleeding sacrificial victim upon the altar. Alert and reverently inquisitive, His young mind sought the meaning of the strange symbolism of this offering of an innocent lamb. No one could tell Him what it meant, not even the priests themselves. The latter mouthed phrases and performed rituals the meaning of which they could not grasp. For four thousand years God's servants had offered the blood of beasts as an atonement for sin. To the Youth's inquiring "Why?" no one could give an answer, nor could anyone explain the mystery of blood sacrifice. Is it possible, wondered Jesus, for the "blood of bulls and goats" to take away sin?

A PRAYER OFFERED IN HEAVEN IS OFFERED AGAIN ON EARTH.

Even as a child, Jesus must walk alone. He turned away from the idle chatter and frivolous play of His companions. Not even His earthly parents could help Him. Silent and alone, He pondered the sight of shed blood that had impressed Him so deeply. Paul tells us what happened in His mind as He came to realize that the blood of goats, calves, or lambs, could never atone for human sin. Not only in heaven before He came, but also as a youth on His knees, He gained an insight and formed the same heart commitment He had made in heaven:

> "For this reason, when Christ was about to come into the world, He said to God: 'You do not want sacrifices and offerings, but You have prepared a body for Me. You are not pleased with animals burned whole on the altar or with sacrifices to take away sins. Then I said, "Here I am, to *do Your* will, O God."'" Hebrews 10:5-7, TEV.

It was as if He prayed: Father, You have no need of all these rivers of beasts' blood! You have no delight in them because they cannot avail to wash away sin from even one human heart. But you have made Me what I am—*I* have a body that I can give! *I* have blood that I can shed.

Here *I* am, Father—let *Me* be the Lamb of God! *I* will die for the sins of the world. *My* blood will be the atonement! *I* will be that "suffering servant" of Isaiah on whom the Lord has laid the iniquity of all. Let *Me* be wounded for man's transgressions, bruised for his iniquities, that with *My* stripes he may be healed. Lo, *I* come—to do Your will, O God!

Paul adds that Jesus took away the Old Testament typical offerings, and established instead the antitypical offering of Himself:

> "So God does away with all the old sacrifices and puts the sacrifice of Christ in their place. Because Jesus Christ did what God wanted Him to do, we are all purified from sin by the offering that He made of His own body once and for all." Hebrews 10:9, 10, TEV.

A BOY'S LOVE (*AGAPE*) BECOMES PROFOUND.

No memory of His preexistence could interpret for Jesus the solemn meaning of that mysterious Passover service. He could not recall the fateful agreement with the eternal Father before the world was, when "the counsel of peace" was "between them both" (Zechariah 6:13), and the Son gave Himself to be the Lamb of God that takes away the sin of the world. His own pure mind, undefiled with sin, gradually discerned the import of what He saw.

It dawned upon Him that these lambs and sacrifices "cannot make him who performed the service perfect in regard to the conscience" (Hebrews 9:9), and that "the law, having a shadow of the good things to come, and not the very image of the things, can never with these same sacrifices, which they offer continually year by year, make those who approach perfect." Hebrews 10:1.

This is all a *type*, He reasoned. Someone innocent, sinless, holy, and undefiled, must die as a Lamb of God if lost human hearts will ever be reached! The whole vain round of types and shadows must be dramatically brought to an end in the offering up of some divine sacrifice.

This was a conclusion that the wise men and priests of Israel in the course of millenniums had not discerned. But now, seeing for the first time what others had witnessed countless times "not discerning the Lord's body," this Boy of twelve understands. Through His youthful soul there surges the unresisted power of a mighty resolve. These poor souls, looking vainly to human efforts for salvation, must not be left mercilessly to what will prove at last only hopeless despair. *He will sacrifice Himself.* The Boy of twelve "saw it, and it displeased Him that there was no justice. He saw that there was no man, and wondered that there was no intercessor; therefore His own arm brought salvation for Him; and His own righteousness, it sustained Him." Isaiah 59:15, 16. "Christ ... through the eternal Spirit offered Himself without spot to God." Hebrews 9:14.

Behold the amazing work of love! He tabernacles in human flesh, a Boy of tender years, with the mysterious past all unknown to Him except by faith in the Written Word. He makes the same decision which as Commander of the heavenly hosts He made in the councils of heaven. *He chooses to go to the cross.*

THE ONLY WAY OUR "LIFE" CAN BE SAVED.

When the love of God (*agape*) is shed abroad in our hearts by the Holy Spirit given to us, we choose the way of the cross as readily as the Son of God chose it in the heavenly council ages ago, and again as a Boy of twelve in the Jerusalem temple. In each instance, whether in the heart of the Son of God or in the heart of a believing sinner, the results lead to resurrection—which is as much a part of the principle as is the cross. There is Good News: "He who hates his life in this world will keep it for life eternal." John 12:25.

There are two crosses: the cross of Christ, and the cross for you and me on which we die with Christ as did the penitent thief.

There was a third cross at Calvary, but there was no redemption for the impenitent thief who died on it. He was caught in a suffering and death to which he never surrendered. Rebellious, he cursed his fate and God unto the bitter end, *and perished.*

Shall we rebel against the principle of the cross and follow him to eternal darkness?

Bearing our cross is made easy through seeing that other cross on which our divine Example died. "My yoke is easy," the crucified One tells us. Through understanding His cross, we can discern our own and find strength to bear it gladly.

> When I survey the wondrous cross
>> On which the Prince of glory died,
> My richest gain I count but loss,
>> And pour contempt on all my pride.
> Were the whole realm of nature mine,
>> That were a tribute far too small;
> Love so amazing, so divine,
>> Demands my life, my soul, my all.
>> ⇝ Isaac Watts

Chapter 6

WHO IS THE "OLD MAN" CRUCIFIED WITH CHRIST?

⌐∽

ADEAR CHRISTIAN WOMAN WAS STRICKEN WITH BLINDNESS. While she lay on her bed trying to sense the meaning of her tragic plight, her well-intentioned pastor called to comfort her.

"Dear one, God has laid His cross upon you!" he said.

How would you feel if someone told you that a misfortune that came to you uninvited was your cross? Would you be tempted to feel resentful toward God for thus interfering with your plans for your life?

No one in his right mind would voluntarily choose the sorrows and heartaches common to humanity which we have so often thought to be our cross. The cross which the Savior bids us bear must be taken up as a freewill choice, just as much so as He took up His cross willingly. No one would choose to become blind, lame, a paraplegic, or even poverty-stricken. While it is good for us to bear these burdens cheerfully, such patient endurance comes short of fulfilling the principle of the cross *as Jesus taught it.*

More than any other of the apostles of Christ, Paul recognized the tremendous impact the cross has on human nature. Not only had he been well educated in Jewish thought; he had mastered also the ideas of Greek philosophy. The startling idea of the cross struck Jews and Greeks differently. To the Jews it was a "stumbling block;" to the Greeks it was "foolishness." 1 Corinthians 1:23.

43

CHRIST'S CROSS IS NO MORE WELCOME TODAY THAN ANCIENTLY.

It is not surprising that the Greeks saw the cross as "foolishness," unenlightened as they were with that wisdom that the Jews ought to have given them. The Greeks had a word for "self"—*ego*. But what to *do* with *egoism,* they hadn't the slightest idea. When Paul came along and said that self must be "crucified," they thought his idea was "nonsense" (TEV).

On the other hand, the idea of a cross was repugnant to the Jews because they were blindly (though inexcusably) ignorant of a psychology of human nature. Had they seen the meaning of their own sanctuary service, they would have recognized in the atonement of Christ the perfect answer to the need of all human nature the world around. But they were pathetically ignorant of the meaning of their own revelation.

Being familiar with Greek philosophy, Paul sensed how "the sons of this world are more shrewd in their generation than the sons of light" (Luke 16:8) in that they at least were aware that human nature needed something which none of the religions of their ancient world supplied. "The Greeks seek after wisdom," Paul said (1 Corinthians 1:22); but he recognized that in the principle of the cross lay the wisdom they were vainly seeking, and which the unconscious repression of human nature had obscured.

PAUL'S UNDERSTANDING OF THE CROSS EXPLAINS LIFE'S GREATEST PROBLEM.

Nothing in the New Testament claims to be a full, systematic outline of the teaching on the cross as Paul presented it to his audiences in Asia Minor. All we have is a collection of occasional letters, none of which Paul intended as a transcript of his ideas which turned the ancient world "upside down." Acts 17:6. Therefore we find in these letters evidence of Paul's dynamic concepts that split history in two.

Much comes to light that shows Paul's vivid idea of the cross as the only way to change selfish human behavior. The clearest explanation is found in his letters to the Roman and Galatian churches:

"Surely you know that when we were baptized into union with Christ Jesus, we were baptized into union with His death. By our baptism, then, we were buried with Him and shared His death, in order that, just as Christ was raised from death by the glorious power of the Father, so also we might live a new life.... Our old being has been put to death with Christ on His cross, in order that the power of the sinful self might be destroyed, so that we should no longer be the slaves of sin. *For when a person dies, he is set free from the power of sin.*" Romans 6:3-7, TEV.

"I have been put to death with Christ on His cross, so that it is no longer I who live, but it is Christ who lives in me." Galatians 2:19, 20, TEV.

The King James Version describes "our old being" as "our old man." He is a strange figure. Who is he?

Is he Satan? Hardly, because Satan will never consent to be crucified with Christ, nor can God force him to be.

Is the "old man" our "sinful nature"? Paul had another term that he used when he spoke of our "sinful nature." He called it "sinful flesh." Romans 8:3. (Obviously, there is nothing sinful about one's flesh in the sense of physical body! "Sinful flesh" is "carnal mind" or "sinful nature." Verse 7. Compare NKJV with TEV.)

Paul's original idea of our "old man" is more than what our "sinful nature" means. What he is talking about is not merely what *appears* to be bad. It may be what we would like to think is a good nature, unenlightened as we are concerning our true spiritual condition. Unless we are very careful we may say, "This must be crucified, but that need not be crucified," when in reality both aspects of our nature alike stem from a love of self. After we are proudly certain that the "sinful nature" has been thoroughly crucified today, tomorrow the "old man" may still be peeking at us from behind the curtains of our self-centered facade.

GETTING DOWN TO THE ROOT OF OUR HUMAN PROBLEM.

For example, our "sinful nature" is thought to be revealed in sinful acts, so that the crucifixion of the "old man" is supposed to consist only of mortifying those *acts* of sin. But Jesus taught that it is the lustful thought, not merely the act, which is the sin of adultery; and cherished hatred even before the act of killing is murder. The sinful nature stems from the existence of the self, or ego. It shows itself in a love for sin. David recognized this truth when he said, "I was brought forth in iniquity, and in sin my mother conceived me." Psalm 51:5.

Sin is therefore not only what we *do,* but what we *are.* Sin is rightly understood to be "transgression of the law" (1 John 3:4, KJV; the word is *anomia,* which means hatred of the law, thus a hatred of God). But it must be remembered that transgression is much deeper than outward acts. The first sin was the cherishing of the "I" in the heart of Lucifer. The last sin of mankind that must be overcome is the same.

In our search to understand who the "old man" is, we are perplexed by another term: what is the "body of sin" which is destroyed when the "old man" is crucified? Is the "body of sin" the same as the "sinful body"?

We know that the physical cravings of our body are sometimes connected with acts of sin. Does that mean that the bodily cravings or instincts are themselves sin? In order to destroy the "body of sin," must we continually repress our physical cravings?

The "body of sin" is not the physical body, but it is the root or source of sin, just as the "body" of this book is the text in the chapters aside from the covers. The "old man" is so important that once he is crucified, the "body of sin," or source and taproot of it, is "destroyed."

WHO IS THE "OLD MAN" WHO IS CRUCIFIED WITH CHRIST?

Paul himself answers our question as simply as we can answer what x is in the equation $x + 2 = 4$. We simply answer: $4 - 2 = 2$; therefore, $x = 2$. In Romans he says the "old man" is crucified with Christ; in Galatians he says that what is crucified with Christ is *I*. Therefore, the "old man" is simply "I," or *self*. In Today's English Version it is translated "the sinful self."

To Paul the truth was as simple and obvious as sunlight: the love of self is the source of all sin; and self cannot be dealt with merely by punishment, beatings, or even denial. It cannot even be ignored. *It must be crucified.*

Forthwith, says Paul, the sin problem is solved, because in dealing with the source, or "body of sin," we have dealt with its taproot. Pull out the root of a tree, and the tree is dead. "He who has died has been freed from sin." Romans 6:7. Understood and accepted, the principle of the cross would go far to solve the psychiatric problems in our modem world as well as in the Greek world of Paul.

BUT HOW IS SELF TO BE CRUCIFIED?

Such an idea would have been worse than foolishness and utter vanity, were we not given an object lesson showing *how* it can be. The cross of Christ is our demonstration. Self can never be crucified by ourselves alone; it must be crucified *with* Christ.

In fact, for self to be crucified *with* Christ is as natural for the heart that believes as it is to say "thank you" to someone who does a gracious deed for us. The way of the cross is not difficult so long as we behold the Lamb of God on His cross. *Seeing* Christ crucified, comprehending what it means, leads to self being crucified with Him. "I, if I am lifted up from the earth, will draw all peoples to Myself." John 12:32.

Satan's favorite scheme therefore is to envelop the cross of Christ in a hazy mist of confusion so that we cannot understand what happened there. He will then be free to taunt us with the supposed impossibility of our bearing our cross: "What foolishness the idea of the cross is in our modern, competitive world! How dare you crucify self? There's nothing you can do but surrender to the popular and universal idea of self-love! Pamper yourself! Get ahead! Walk over others!" So the enemy would bombard us everyday.

If the cross of Christ is hidden, Satan is right; without the clear vision of Christ crucified, there is nothing any of us can do but do but live unto self.

But let Christ's cross emerge out of the mists, and it becomes the "power of God" (1 Corinthians 1:18) to all who appreciate its worth.

THE CLARITY OF THE TRUTH.

No involved, difficult, or obscure process of doing battle with sin is the method of God. His plan is simplicity itself. In fact, sin itself is as simple a thing as God's remedy for overcoming it—indulged love of self. Kneeling before the throne of God as the "anointed cherub who covers" (Ezekiel 28:14), Lucifer did not appreciate or love the principles of God's self-denying character. His heart was lifted up with his own beauty, and his wisdom was corrupted by reason of his brightness. Verse 17. This lack of appreciation for the character of God is what the Bible calls "unbelief." It is the precondition of sin. From that root in the heart of Lucifer came all the pride and passion of sin as we know it.

The "old man" simply being the cherished "I," or self, it dies with Christ when the love revealed at the cross is seen for what it is. Christ has come in our flesh, your flesh, my flesh; He meets our problem of life precisely as we find it. Directly from our given situation wherein we find ourselves, His honesty, His purity, His selflessness, His love, His self-surrender, led Him to His cross. He takes the raw materials of our present life and adds the ingredient of love (*agape*). The result: His cross.

Christ crucified is simply *you* crucified if you have that kind of love. If you had love, you could no more evade the cross than could He have evaded it. When you see that He has come in your flesh, that is, has taken your place in your particular situation at this moment, you can see how love is set straight on the collision course of the cross.

As readily as you say "thank you" for a kindness done you, your heart responds with a deep sense of contrition. All your petty self-love stands revealed in its ugliness. As in ultraviolet light, all the motives of your heart suddenly appear different from what you ever saw them before. No preaching has done the trick—you have *seen* something yourself. What you have seen in that light is the real you, the you that is without love. A light shines from the cross that illuminates your soul in the floodlights of heaven, and you see yourself as the beings of the unfallen universe look upon you.

And now it seems that every character-sinew and cell of your being stands out saturated with that sin of self-love. You feel as if you want to hide your face. But as this strange light of love bathes your soul, every little root of pride and self-esteem shrivels up. The sense of guilt that rises in the heart would kill you outright were it not that Christ already bears that guilt on His cross. You are never crucified alone, but you are crucified with Him. You live, but nevertheless the "old man" dies. Your love of self, your pride, your smug satisfaction with yourself, are shattered—well, there is no better word for it than "crucified."

AND THE TASK OF CONQUERING SIN IS DONE.

No offerings of penance, no expensive pilgrimages to Rome or here or there, no beating yourself or starving yourself, no wearing hair-cloth, no grim gritting your teeth to shake off evil habit after evil habit while you tick off a check-list of assumed "progress." "He that has died has been freed from sin." The atonement of Christ does it; and nothing else in the wide universe can do it.

The best that any other so-called cure for the problem of egoism can accomplish is to suppress the symptoms in one place while they break out afresh in another place, to our embarrassment. So long as the root (the "body of sin") is there intact, we can lop off all the branches we like, but the love of self will go on bearing its fruit of passion, anxiety, worry, envy, lust, and even subtler pride.

But now Christ has drawn you by being uplifted before you. You sense the power in that drawing. Consider it well, for it is the power of love. It is stronger than the mightiest brute forces of nature. It is the principle of God's free universe. Look for yourself, realize for yourself. You don't need to take anyone else's word for anything!

> Was it for crimes that I have done
> He groaned upon the tree?
> Amazing pity! grace unknown!
> And love beyond degree!
>
> Well might the sun in darkness hide,
> And shut his glories in,
> When Christ, the mighty Maker, died
> For man, the creature's, sin.
>
> Thus might I hide my blushing face,
> While His dear cross appears,
> Dissolve my heart in thankfulness,
> And melt mine eyes to tears.
>
> But drops of grief can ne'er repay
> The debt of love I owe;
> Here, Lord, I give myself away;
> 'Tis all that I can do.
>
> ↜ Isaac Watts

Chapter 7

THE SUBTLE REBIRTH OF THE "OLD MAN"

⌒

*U*NLESS CHRIST DIED FOR NOTHING, HIS FOLLOWERS WILL SHINE IN THIS DARK WORLD LIKE STARS ON A BLACK, STORMY NIGHT. They will be free from the curse of selfishness.

But as we look both about us and in us, we see that often when sin is overcome on lower levels, it subtly reappears on higher levels. Selfishness crops out anew, disguised and refined but nonetheless evil. The pathetic pretensions of "saints" who have forgotten that they are sinners have been the scandal and reproach of much that the world sees as "Christianity." Is it hard to imagine the shame that Christ must often feel?

In Jesus' clear teaching about the cross we find the solution to this problem: "Then He said to them all, 'If anyone desires to come after Me, let him deny himself, and take up his cross *daily,* and follow Me.'" Luke 9:23. The reason for Jesus' command to take up our cross *daily* is the fact that the "old man" who was crucified yesterday reappears in a new form today. His true identity is never fully apprehended by the sincere believer.

What we sense as "self" today may be correct, and our experience of renouncing and crucifying self today may be genuine. But each succeeding victory is that of a battle and not the war itself. The "old man" reappears in a higher, more cleverly disguised form daily. Hence the need, as Jesus says, for bearing the cross daily.

CAN WE EVER GET BEYOND BEARING THE CROSS?

If we say Yes, we make ourselves better than Jesus was, because He *had* to fight the battle daily throughout His life. "I do not seek My own will," He said of His daily conflict, "but the will of the Father who sent Me." John 5:30. Jesus would not ask us to follow Him in taking up our cross daily unless He also took up His cross daily. "A disciple is not above his teacher, nor a servant above his master." Matthew 10:24.

Not only will the cross be carried here in this life daily, but even in heaven's eternity the principle of self-renunciation symbolized by the cross will motivate the behavior of the redeemed, while the cross of Christ will remain their study. The book of Revelation presents to us that after sin is no more, Christ will still bear His title as the Crucified One—the "Lamb." The temple in the New Jerusalem is the Lamb; and proceeding from the throne of the Lamb is the river of water of life. The throne of God is the throne of the Lamb. Revelation 21:22; 22:1, 3. The love so amply demonstrated on the cross will ever be recognized as the basis of God's government, and will flow out to all the universe in unending streams of light and life and gladness.

Only as the selfless love of Christ on the cross reigns in every heart will it be certain that sin can never appear again. Should the love of self ever arise in any heart in the universe, the very essence of sin would be back again, and the whole sad war in the universe would have to be repeated. Thank God, that will not happen! "Affliction will not rise up a second time." Nahum 1:9. And in bearing our cross daily now, we are beginning to live out that principle of eternal life. In fact, eternal life begins now.

THERE ARE NEW FORMS THE "OLD MAN" ASSUMES.

Since Jesus' command to take up our cross daily is necessary only because the "old man" is resurrected daily, it is now our duty to discover what new forms the "old man" assumes from day to day.

■ The "old man" may be a polished, refined, highly cultured self, well educated and honorable.

■ He may have excellent tastes in art, literature, and music, and move in the best social circles. But there is no real difference between what we think of as a reprehensible "old man" and this highly cultured, proud self, except that the latter may be more difficult to apprehend and bring to the cross.

■ The "old man" may be fond of doing good works in his family or community.

■ He may enjoy civic leadership, joining idealist clubs, laboring all the time to do a good work while he fails to see the best work. Politicians do a great amount of good; and there are among them many good men and women. But how easily the plaudits of men become a cherished laurel wreath, and pride becomes the reward of service. The "old man" bears away the victory.

■ The most difficult form the "old man" assumes is that of the religious self, finding an outlet for his sinful pride in pious praying, exhorting, and even preaching. Spiritual pride is enhanced by the very sacrifices self makes.

■ In fact, no one needs more carefully to guard against the subtle rebirth of the "old man" than the gospel minister. The performance of his duties, even so-called evangelism, can become most deadly stumbling blocks to real fellowship with Christ if the principle of the cross is not accepted daily.

■ Such labor wrought in self becomes fatal because it is a sinful, self-seeking expression of the "old man's" existence.

This is the reason why the Lord Jesus will be obliged to disclose startling tragedies in the last day: "Many will say to Me in that day, 'Lord, Lord, have we not prophesied in Your name, cast out demons in Your name, and done many wonders in Your name?' And then I will declare to them, 'I never knew you; depart from Me, you who practice lawlessness!'" Matthew 7:22, 23. They had worked evil because it was self that worked.

ALL THAT SELF DOES IS DEADLY SIN.

Since the preaching of the cross is the "power of God" (1 Corinthians 1:18), any preaching which denies the principle of the cross can be nothing else than Satan trying to edge his way in, with the "old man" acting as his agent.

When self does the work, the "old man" is sure that he has been doing it in Christ's name, as Jesus said that "many" would protest to Him in the last day that all the good they had done was done in His name.

Those "many" to whom the Lord must at last deny personal knowledge are a pitiable group. They have felt so sure all along that they were enlisted in Christ's service. They have been ready to praise the Lord for the wonderful works accomplished, not realizing that their confidence was dependent on the results they thought *they* saw. They saw their work, not Christ. The "old man" lives by sight and not by faith.

They have ever been ready to praise the Lord for the wonderful work they have accomplished, but they have not discerned their pride in their hidden thought that the Lord was fortunate enough to have *them* on hand to enable Him do it. Sometimes the deception is so cruel that even the "very elect" are sorely tempted.

Jesus foresaw this subtle temptation when He tenderly pleaded with the disciples not to yield to the insidious pride of spiritual labor. It was when "the seventy returned with joy, saying, 'Lord, even the demons obeyed us when we gave them a command in Your name'" (Luke 10:17, TEV), that Jesus' mind flashed back to the original sin in Lucifer's heart in heaven when he was a minister, even the "anointed cherub who covers."

He quickly saw how easily the excitement of the disciples' rich success could become as Lucifer's pride. "Jesus answered them: 'I saw Satan fall like lightning from heaven. Listen! … Don't be glad because the evil spirits obey you; rather be glad because your names are written in heaven.'" Luke 10:18-20, TEV. If Jesus' words were more heeded by pastors, evangelists, bishops, and other church administrators, how many sincere ministers might be able to overcome the deceptive pressures of ministerial pride!

PAUL HAD A DEEP INSIGHT INTO THIS POSSIBILITY OF TRAGEDY.

He tells us of his conviction that should the gospel worker be willing to confess his "work" a failure *before* the last day, "he himself will be saved yet so as through fire." 1 Corinthians 3:15. Only through such an experience of humbling of heart before God can one be enabled to build upon the foundation a lifework of "gold, silver, precious stones" that shall endure the "fire" of ultimate judgment. Verses 12, 13.

All work founded on anything other than Jesus Christ will prove at last to be only "wood, hay, straw." Verses 12, 15. George MacDonald has said, "Nothing saves a man more than the burning of his work, except the doing of work that can stand in the fire." —*Unspoken Sermons,* page 147.

■ It is easy for the "old man" to covet the honors that follow religious service, especially within a community of people professing to be "spiritual Israel." With them, the seeking of worldly fame and honor has been supposedly "crucified" and there are no opportunities for gratifying the human craving for worldly preeminence. If the "old man" is not crucified daily, his craving for eminence is sublimated in a desire to be an honored leader in the gaze of the limited religious community. As the church increases in prestige and glitz, her "prophets" are thus more and more liable to the deceptive snare of a modem species of Baal worship—self-worship disguised as worship of Christ.

THE "OLD MAN" IS EVEN MORE CRUEL IN HIS DECEPTIONS.

■ Another manifestation the "old man" may assume is that of trust in the rapturous ecstasy of a glorious experience, the miraculous movings of a supernatural power in us and through us.

■ The temptation is strong to regard miracles as proof of the blessing of God. How could the "old man" be involved in a miracle demonstration? Would not denial of miracle power be a denial of God? Not necessarily.

It is not beyond the power of the fallen Lucifer to work miracles. "No wonder! For Satan himself transforms himself into an angel of light."

2 Corinthians 11:14. Are we so sure that we can unerringly distinguish from the genuine work of the Holy Spirit the work of such an "angel of light"? "Let him who thinks he stands take heed lest he fall." 1 Corinthians 10:12.

Our Saviour has kindly warned us: "False christs and false prophets will rise and show great signs and wonders to deceive, if possible, even the elect." Matthew 24:24.

■ Answers to prayer can seem such bona fide evidence of God's special favor and activity on our behalf that we may not realize how much the "old man" is enjoying the experience of pride that seems to lift us above our fellowmen. Dropping names is a common example of one's pride in knowing the high and mighty in this world; the poor fellow who doesn't know these great people is left to wallow in his envy.

■ Pride in one's answers to prayer can likewise arise from one's assumption that he is, like the Pharisees of old, a favorite of Heaven, someone better than the common run of humanity who seem to be denied these miraculous demonstrations in their honor. The part that self played in the glorious experience is not easily discerned.

THE CROSS BECOMES THE BASIS FOR FINAL JUDGMENT.

Look again at that pathetic group who in the judgment remonstrate with Christ, "Have we not prophesied in Your name, cast out demons in Your name, and done many wonders in Your name?" Doubtless they have always *assumed* that their works were done in answer to their prayers in Christ's name. They prayed; and they received undeniable results that were astounding to everybody. But it is clear that the answers to their prayers were not from Christ at all, because He is obliged to tell them sadly, "I never knew you." Matthew 7:22, 23.

Somebody knew them, because there were undeniable miracles in answer to their prayers. If Jesus says that it was not *He* who knew them, who could it have been?

We have seen that Satan has the power to appear as an "angel of light," a "false christ" who "performs great signs." Indeed, he seems to have a connection with heaven, "so that he even makes fire come down from heaven on the earth in the sight of men." But his real character lies concealed in these miracles. John adds that he "deceives those who dwell on the earth by those signs which he was granted to do in the sight of the beast." Revelation 13:13, 14. *Miracles are thus no test of genuine Christian experience.*

■ Nothing may be more difficult to recognize as honor for the "old man" than the rapturous ecstasy of a glorious experience, the psychic movings of some supernatural power in us and through us. But signs and wonders are becoming the peculiar stock in trade of the false christ, or Baal in his modern form.

If it is possible for the "old man" of self to reappear in gospel preaching and ministry, it is also possible for Baal to bless and prosper his prophets in their work. The "christ" of our feelings, or our emotions, is not infallible, but the Christ of the Bible, of the cross, of truth, is infallible. The two must not be confused!

> The last temptation is the greatest treason:
> To do the right deed for the wrong reason.
> ↩ T. S. Eliot, *Murder in the Cathedral*

Either Christ or Satan will be the eventual object of every soul's heart service, with no middle ground possible in the final crisis yet to come. Since Satan well knows that but few will ever knowingly and openly choose his service, he is obliged to make it *appear* that the worship of self is the worship of Christ, because it is in man's devotion to self that Satan claims as allegiance to his principles. This is the genius of the "antichrist."

Skillfully he is preparing for the last great conflict, hoping to sweep into his ranks the multitudes of earth, including the "elect" through the avenue of a devotion to self which appears on the surface to be devotion to Christ. Many will not discern that their very motive of service has been either a desire for reward for themselves, or a craven fear of punishment. Like a fickle populace in the changing fortunes of war, they were ready to submit to whoever offers in his hand the prizes of reward or wields the sword of power, irrespective of a genuine appreciation of his character.

■ The "old man" will obsequiously submit to whoever has the upper hand.

BUT CHRIST WILL ACCEPT NO SUCH SERVICE BASED ON FORCE.

There must, therefore, come a test to every soul to prove his/her deepest heart devotion. That test is one's response to the way of the cross. Day by day the test continues.

When one is sick or injured, proper medical care may sometimes involve painful experiences. But no one in his right mind will refuse the pain that leads to health and renewed life.

The way of the cross is likewise a health-giving experience. The "deceitfulness of sin" may make the bearing of the cross seem unpleasant, but when one is brought up "out of a horrible pit, out of the miry clay," and one's feet are "set … upon a rock," joy follows the pain as surely as day follows night. The "rock" is Christ and the "miry clay" is the constant bewilderment and confusion of domination by the "old man" of self and sensuality. Psalm 40:1, 2.

Are you weary of your fear, your killing anxiety, your envy of others, your sense of insecurity, your haunting awareness of vanity?

Let your feet be set on that solid rock where the cross is planted. What joy will be yours to say, "He … has put a new song in my mouth—praise to our God!" Verse 3.

> The Lord is my light, then why should I fear?
> By day and by night His presence is near.
> He is my salvation from sorrow and sin.
> This blessed persuasion the Spirit brings in.
>
> ⌐ James Nicholson

Chapter 8

JESUS' THIRD LESSON ON THE MEANING OF THE CROSS

⤴

JESUS FELT THE TREMENDOUS TEMPTATION OF HIS GREAT POPULARITY. Should He ride the crest of the wave that was mounting upward, bearing Him prominently to the pinnacle of national prestige and influence?

Or should He arrest the movement of popularity by solemnly announcing the real truth of His Messianic message—His coming sacrifice on the cross?

This was no mystic secret reserved for the inner circle of a few close disciples. At the height of His ministry when "great multitudes went with Him," He boldly proclaimed to them all the same testing truth. Luke reveals how He chose to present it with ultra simple realism to the startled ears of the "great multitude":

> "And He turned, and said to them, 'If anyone comes to Me and does not hate his father and mother, wife and children, brothers and sisters, yes, and his own life also, he cannot be My disciple. And whoever does not bear his cross and come after Me cannot be My disciple.'" Luke 14:25-27.

It was as if He said, I am glad to see you following Me; but are you really sure this is your heart's choice? I must be plainly honest with you. I am indeed the Messiah, but not the one of popular hopes and expectations. I am indeed going to the kingdom of heaven, but mark you, My route lies via the cross. If you follow Me, you must of necessity accept My route. Many will at some future time mistake the god of this world for the Christ; I must ensure now that you do not mistake the Christ for the god of this world.

IT REQUIRES RARE PREACHING, SELDOM HEARD TODAY, TO LEAVE THE HEARERS THUS FREE TO DECIDE.

But Jesus had no fear of the multitudes. He had faithfully preached the truth—so faithfully, in fact, that His path was leading Him directly to His own death. Why then need He fear to present the cross to the multitudes and to call for their decision? Only the man who himself bears the cross dare summon others to do so. What need had Christ to resort to any psychological subterfuge? The way of the cross had delivered Him from any such helpless vanity.

Since it is clear that a decision to accept the gospel is a decision to accept the cross, and since that decision can be made only by the inner heart of hearts, it follows that there must be no confusing pressure in true soul-winning work. Simple truth needs no alluring embellishments to make it attractive to the honest heart.

In fact, such embellishments serve only to repulse the sincere seeker for truth who fails to discern the voice of the True Shepherd in the confusing appeals to "self" voiced by the would-be soul winner. Psychological tricks and egocentric inducements to "decision" can be the tool only of one who knows not the strength of the cross.

The reason the cross is the "power of God unto salvation" is that love alone has true drawing power. "I have loved you with an everlasting love; therefore with lovingkindness I have drawn you." Jeremiah 31:3.

George Mattheson, author of the beautiful hymn "O Love That Wilt Not Let Me Go," has made the following apt comment:

> "I understand the word 'drawn' to be used here as of the opposite of 'driven.' I take the meaning to be: 'It is because I love you that I do not force you; I desire to win by love.' Love is incompatible with the exercise of omnipotence. Inexorable law can rule the stars; but the stars are not an object of love. Man is an object of love, and therefore he can only be ruled by love, as the prophet puts it, 'drawn.' Nothing is a conquest for love but the power of love, of drawing. Omnipotence can subdue by driving, but that is not a conquest for love; it is rather a sign that love is baffled.
>
> "Therefore it is that our Father does not compel us to come in. He would have us drawn by the beauty of holiness; therefore He veils all that would force the will. He hides the glories of heaven. He conceals the gates of pearl and the streets of gold. He reveals not the river of His pleasures. He curtains from the ear the music of the upper choir. He obscures in the sky the sign of the Son of man. He forbids the striking of the hours on the clock of eternity. He treads on a path of velvet lest the sound of His coming footsteps should conquer by fear the heart that ought to be won by love."—*Thoughts for Life's Journey,* pages 70, 71.

CHRIST WOULD RATHER *DRAW* BY THE CROSS THAN *DRIVE* BY THE CROWN.
The converts who come by way of the cross are those whom the Father draws. In His mysterious process of drawing, He doesn't want mere lip servers, but disciples who will *follow* the Lamb wherever He goes. The power of the drawing is in the truth, for Christ is the Truth. If truth

is made unmistakable, the power will prove to be invincible. Another way of saying the same thing is that the truth-seeker and truth are made for each other and when they meet, like Crazy Glue they unite.

On the other hand, the use of psychological and emotional techniques designed to force "decision" may attract an entirely wrong class of adherents who are neither disciples nor followers of the Lamb. If "decision" is secured on the basis of naked self-interest, it cannot be of faith. And "whatever is not of faith is sin." Romans 14:23. In the resultant confusion, the True Shepherd's "sheep" may be turned away completely because "they will by no means follow a stranger, but will flee from him, for they do not know the voice of strangers." John 10:5. This may be one reason why sometimes so few people respond to gospel invitations.

Putting a stumbling block before Christ's "little ones" is surely sin. But Jesus said that His own sheep hear His voice. "The sheep follow Him, for they know His voice." "My own know Me, as the Father knows Me and I know the Father." John 10:3, 4, 14, 15, RSV. Those "other sheep" of Christ's fold therefore need not be *persuaded* to accept gospel truth; once the truth (made known by the voice of Christ) is clearly presented to them, no power in earth or hell can possibly *dissuade* them from following that Voice!

The winsomeness is in the truth itself because love and truth are inseparable. He who thinks he is speaking right doctrine but does not speak in love cannot be speaking truth.

CAN THE LOVE OF SELF ALSO INCLUDE LOVE OF FAMILY?

If Jesus' words to the multitudes sound a bit hard, we must know that He was not teaching an attitude of harsh, unfeeling hatred toward one's loved ones in the family circle. The biblical meaning of the word "hate" is to love less in comparison.

An illustration of what He meant can be found in His attitude toward His own mother and relatives. He tenderly loved His mother, and even in His desperate hour on the cross was thoughtful of her needs. His was a perfect example of filial devotion. However, He would permit no family tie, however intimate, to lessen His devotion to all suffering, needy members of the human family.

On one occasion while He was helping the multitudes, His relatives arrived: "Then His mother and brothers came to Him, and could not approach Him because of the crowd. And it was told Him by some, who said, 'Your mother and Your brothers are standing outside, desiring to see You.' But He answered and said to them, 'My mother and My brothers are these who hear the word of God and do it.'" Luke 8:19-21.

Here was no spurning of the tender affections of kin, but rather a recognition that these affections must not become perverted through a failure to love *all* needy members of the human family. It is a deep lesson that many of us need to grasp, who instinctively feel that our charity can be confined within the narrow walls enclosing precious kinfolk or close friends.

Love of family and pride of blood can be a very difficult form the "old man" assumes. When God calls us to do something or to go somewhere for Him, and we say No because of the ties of kinship that bind us, here is the "old man" alive and well. Love for those who *potentially* will "hear the word of God, and do it" will prevail even as Jesus heeded the call to come to save us. But when a call comes to leave father, mother, brother, sister, and other cherished ties of the homeland, to go to a distant land in service for Christ, "self" often protests. Seldom is it seen that rejection of duty is a rejection of the cross.

JESUS' ENTIRE LIFE WAS DEVOTED TO SERVICE, EVEN FROM CHILDHOOD.

It was His to "taste" all the suffering and privation that we humans can know. Although many rejected Him, there were those who listened to the voice of the Holy Spirit and were drawn to Him. And there were worshipers of "self" who belonged to Satan's kingdom who did not respond to the drawing. Eventually all would show on which side they stood.

And thus throughout time everyone passes judgment on himself.

There will be a day of final judgment when every lost person will understand why he is "outside." In the final encounter, as on a screen, the cross will be presented, and its real bearing will be seen by every mind that has been blinded by sin. When the lost see Calvary with its mysterious Victim, sinners will condemn themselves. People will see what their final choice was been.

If we refuse a call to difficult service for our Master because of love of family or for other selfish reasons, there can be no lighter sentence awaiting us eventually than if we reject Bible truth for similar excuses. In either case it is the cross which is being rejected rather than either doctrine or service.

THERE IS A "PRICE" TO PAY IN BUILDING CHARACTER.

In explaining the cross to the multitudes Jesus used three simple illustrations.

(1) The first shows the need for counting the cost before one professes the building of Christian character. The price to be paid is the bearing of the cross:

> "If one of you is planning to build a tower, he sits down first and figures out what it will cost, to see if he has enough money to finish the job. If he doesn't, he will not be able to finish the tower after laying the foundation; and all who see what happened will make fun of him. 'This man began to build but can't finish the job!' they will say." Luke 14:28-30, TEV.

There was something decidedly attractive in the teaching of Christ. Its appeal was phenomenal. But Jesus saw that this very appeal, in the warmth of its rushing tide, might sweep the emotions into impulsive beginnings of character-building which would bring shame if left unfinished. The irresistible rush of enthusiastic devotion will be needed later when the cost has been counted and accepted. *For the cost is the cross.*

Accept the "price" first; *then* let the tide of emotional appeal reinforce the consecration. Understand at the outset, Jesus said in effect, that the cross on which self is crucified is the price for the building of any useful and enduring Christian character. Failure to count the cost of surrender to the cross brings a disgraceful failure to reach the proper heights of Christian character. An unfinished "tower" can result only in the grief of heaven, the scornful derision of the world, and a painful shame of disillusionment for the builder.

How often has the world laughed at the inconsistencies of professed followers of the Lamb. Perhaps the early enthusiasm gave promise of a wonderful edifice to be erected. After the early difficulties with gross evils such as drunkenness, tobacco, sensuality, and the like, it is assumed that the work will be carried on to completion.

But there comes a time when subtle evils impede further progress. Gradually the "workmen" on the "tower" are withdrawn, and the heart is left an unfinished temple marred with deficiencies, unsightly in its deformity. Pride, evil temper, catty impatience, pious selfishness, uncharitable judgment, peevishness, envy—these constitute the ruins of an unfinished character. "All who see what happened will make fun of him. 'This man began to build but can't finish the job!'" Christ is dishonored in His professed follower.

The "builder" himself can miss out on both worlds through a failure to reckon the true cost of Christian experience. A painful sense of futility comes to anyone who has used all his resources in a half-finished building program. Few have the courage to tear down the unfinished "tower" that the embarrassment of failure might be hidden through ceasing to profess Christ. Most are content, like survivors in bombed houses, to dwell in the dismal rubble, hoping that sometime resources for the completion of the "tower" will be miraculously forthcoming. Such hopes are doomed to ultimate disappointment unless we here and now assess the cost and surrender to its payment.

When the "tower" of Christlike character is properly finished, the world will see it and marvel. There can be no power more effective for the finishing of the gospel commission in the earth than the finishing of that work in our own hearts.

MEASURING THE STRENGTH OF THE ENEMY, AS IN WAR.

(2) The second illustration Jesus gave was that of the unequal battle:

> "'If a king goes out with ten thousand men to fight another king who comes against him with twenty thousand men, he will sit down first and decide if he is strong enough to face that other king. If he isn't, he will have to send messengers to meet the other king to ask for terms of peace while he is still a long way off. In the same way,' concluded Jesus, 'none of you can be My disciple unless he gives up everything he has.'" Luke 14:31-33, TEV.

Solemn words!

Human nature sees the futility of a king seeking battle with an army twice as strong as his own. Any king with sense would send messengers to seek out the best terms possible, salvage as much of the original kingdom as he could, and then abandon the rest. The invader dictates the terms he will impose and sets the new boundaries. On one side he sets up his new kingdom; on the other, the overmastered king will dwell with his trembling subjects, trying vainly to keep up a pretense of the old glory and power, while his independence is gone.

Jesus was here illustrating the solemn truths of the cross.

In effect, He was saying: Do not underestimate the strength of the enemy with whom you strive, namely, the "old man," or "self." If your will to crucify self is only half as strong as the will of the "old man" to live, you must be reduced to the pitiable recourse of seeking a truce. Better have the courage to forsake all. Only thus can you defeat the enemy. Be My disciple in truth, and rejoice in your freedom and victory.

BUT HOW MANY MAKE A TRUCE WITH THE ENEMY!

The heart is divided with a boundary. Feebly, a show of loyalty is kept up by attendance at divine worship, tithe paying, and participation in some Christian endeavor of good works. The boundary divides the kingdom of the "old man" from that of his puppet. The "old man" dwells on one side, the halfhearted Christian on the other. There are occasional border incidents, for it is a kind of armed frontier. The soul cannot rest. But if one is unwilling to risk an all-out engagement, he must dwell side by side with the enemy.

Jesus' apt illustration shows the Laodicean condition of lukewarmness. It is a state neither radiantly alive, nor dead, but in between—pitifully weak; neither hot nor cold, lukewarm.

WE CANNOT FOREVER REMAIN IN SUCH TEPID DEVOTION.

Eventually reality must be faced. We come to the point of decision, the dividing of the ways. We must choose one of two roads— one leading back to Egypt and apostasy, the other leading by way of the cross to the sunlit plains of the heavenly Canaan and eternal victory. Which will we choose?

Patience and so-called balance can be overdone in our time of crisis. The former can degenerate into cowardice, and the latter, when thermostatic, can be most disappointing to our Saviour. He knew no lukewarm "balance" in His love which drove Him to His cross. "My devotion to Your house, O God, burns in Me like a fire," He says. John 2:17, TEV. Peter Marshall prayed, "While time is running out, save us from patience which is akin to cowardice. Give us the courage to be either hot or cold, to stand for something, lest we fall for anything."

THERE IS A HIDDEN ELEMENT OF VALUE.

(3) The third illustration Jesus gave about the cross is striking in its simplicity:

> "Salt is good, but if it loses its saltiness, there is
> no way to make it salty again. It is no good for the soil or
> for the manure pile; it is thrown away." Luke 14:34, 35, TEV.

Christianity is good. But if that Christianity has lost the principle of the cross, what is it good for? It is fit only for what is happening to it in many parts of the world. It is not execrated, cast on the "manure pile" through persecution and violent opposition; nor yet is it valued as the world's only vital preservative as it should be. It is merely ignored, trodden underfoot, "thrown away."

Those good people who comprise the church of Jesus are indeed the salt of the earth. But the saltiness which alone can cause them to preserve the world from spoiling prematurely must be seen for what it is. Moral rot will corrupt the whole world unless that saltiness is in God's people. What is needed is the preaching, and the living of the principle, of the cross!

Solemnly Jesus warned the chosen people of His day of the danger of their not discerning a hidden lack in their work for their world. To the outward eye and touch, whole mountains of salt may appear beautiful, glistening white, and genuine. Enraptured souls may exclaim regarding the marvelous potential of such an abundance of "salt" for salting the needy earth. But an increase in volume and weight of such salt is no increase to its saltiness. Numerical and statistical increases to the church do not necessarily make her any more the "salt of the earth." Tons upon tons of salt that has lost its savor is worth less than a cup of truly salty salt.

There were neither refrigerators nor ice storage facilities in the world of Jesus two millennia ago. Salt was used as the preservative for meat and fish. A shipment packed in saltless salt spoiled.

The spoilage process in the moral and spiritual health of our world today is plain for anyone to see and feel for himself. Brutal ethnic cleansings and genocides are terrifying. Crime, the inroads of loveless infidelity, the corruption of human morality, the steady degeneration of physical and mental vitality—all are alarming evidence that our sinful world is spoiling like rotten fish on the way to market.

It was never God's plan that the world spoil for want of salty salt to preserve it. He never intended that the work of His followers should be made so difficult in these last days. The final conflict between Christ and Satan could take place without the need for moral and spiritual values to degenerate to the place that multitudes become unable to comprehend the gospel sufficiently to accept or reject it intelligently.

In His love and mercy, God intends that His last message to the world shall be considered thoughtfully and freely by a world population capable of *intelligent* acceptance or rejection. In His providence His people are scattered all over the world among many nations, tongues, and peoples. Their living the principles of the cross, with their proclamation of its message, is to be a preservative salt to a society that will otherwise spoil to a desperate degradation without it.

But let us take heart. The world will surely listen to the message of the cross when presented in its "high-fidelity" truth. Even the obvious fact that much preaching is ignored can be a cause for encouragement, for it is not genuine Christianity that the world so ignores, but merely the crossless imitation of it. No *salty* salt is ever "trodden underfoot." It will be accepted vigorously, or rejected vigorously.

So it was in the days of Christ and His apostles; and so will it be until history ends.

Jesus concluded His sermon to the multitudes:

"Listen, then, if you have ears!"

Chapter 9

HOW I DISCOVERED THE CROSS

∽

WHEN I WAS A YOUTH I HEARD THE STORY OF THE CROSS OF JESUS, WITH ALL THE HARROWING DETAILS. I had also heard stories of martyrs who had died in the Dark Ages for their faith. My young mind found it hard to distinguish between the suffering Jesus endured on His cross and that endured by the faithful martyrs.

In fact, it seemed that some of the tortures the martyrs endured might have been even more painful than Jesus' flogging and crucifixion, and longer in duration as well.

As I became older, I began to appreciate a little more the more-than-physical pain of His sufferings. I could sense the shame and loneliness He had to endure. His disciples and friends all forsook Him and fled, whereas most of the martyrs had at least someone to cheer them in their last hours. But still I found it difficult to see how Christ's sufferings were more severe than those of some people I could imagine suffered both excruciating physical torture and the loneliness of rejection.

It also seemed to me that anyone could better endure unpleasantness and pain if he could look forward to a bright future of reward. I had learned that when a person died, if he were good he went to heaven for such a reward; and if he were bad, to an opposite place of torture and punishment. Jesus was undeniably good. Therefore, I reasoned to myself, as soon as He died He must have gone straight to heaven for an enjoyable weekend in reunion with His Father and the angels. The

71

assurance that He was going there seemed expressed in the promise to the dying thief, "Today you will be with Me in Paradise." Luke 23:43.

Jesus died about three o'clock Friday afternoon and was resurrected early Sunday morning. I assumed therefore He must have spent the intervening time in heaven or at least Paradise, whatever that was. Such an anticipation could well have buoyed up His spirits during His severe trials. It is almost incredible what people can endure when they are certain of an almost immediate reward. Where was the unique "glory" in Christ's cross?

Further, the length of time during which He suffered His physical pain did not seem to be long. All the floggings and the final agony hardly lasted more than twelve or fifteen hours. Long enough, indeed; I shouldn't want to endure such pain for a fraction of that time. But many people have been forced to endure torture for longer periods, and without the hope of an imminent happy weekend such as I supposed Christ looked forward to.

TRY AS I COULD, I FOUND IT DIFFICULT TO SEE ANYTHING
VERY WONDERFUL IN JESUS' CROSS.

Perhaps, I thought, what makes it so special is the fact that the Sufferer was the Son of God enduring all these agonies we poor humans must sometimes know. I could sense a certain feeling of awe, much as I would feel if a king were to condescend to sleep under our family roof, toil in our garden with us, and eat at our humble table. I could look and wonder, but I could hardly understand.

It troubled me that I could not induce within myself those feelings of deep heart appreciation for the cross that others have seemed to feel. According to what I had heard, I should "glory" in the cross of Christ, feel some unusual emotion or profound movings of heart. I saw some people actually moved to tears about it. I felt worried because I couldn't.

It seemed I couldn't touch with my fingertips what Paul sensed when he said, "God forbid that I should glory except in the cross of our Lord Jesus Christ." Galatians 6:14.

I TRIED VERY HARD TO BE IMPRESSED AS I THOUGHT
I SHOULD BE IMPRESSED.

But I couldn't help reasoning that if the Sufferer were the Son of God, knowledge of that fact should certainly have made it easier for Him to endure trials that to us in our finiteness and partial ignorance seem so distressing and painful. He knew all things, He knew that He had "come from God and went to God." Surely He could stand for a short time the physical discomforts and pain we know for long periods of time! What is so wonderful?

I remembered reading an experience of a man who was once one of the world's richest men—Henry Ford, the builder of both the once-famous "Model T" and the luxurious Lincoln automobiles. Traveling incognito with a party of friends on some back roads, Mr. Ford had whimsically chosen to drive one of his little Model T's. It broke down—an event many of his less wealthy customers also experienced—and he was obliged to seek repairs at a village garage. Although he was inconvenienced a short time, the story indicated that he thoroughly enjoyed the experience. I felt sure that one reason was his inner knowledge that he didn't have to depend on that balky Model T to get him home. Any moment he wished he could have telegraphed for a fleet of his Lincoln limousines to come and rescue him. With confidence others could not know, Mr. Ford might have enjoyed what the ordinary motorist of that day would have endured only with much anxiety.

Wasn't Christ in much the same situation? I reasoned. At any moment in His trials He told Peter He could pray to His Father and He would send Him more than twelve legions of angels. Matthew 26:53. A soldier in bulletproof armor should be expected to show more courage than one without it.

AND "SAVED BY FAITH" PERPLEXED ME.

I had heard it said that we are saved by faith. But I apparently couldn't get it. Was there something wrong with me, or had God given me the brush-off, leaving me to be lost for want of a proper appreciation of what His Son had done for me? Or should I force myself to say I felt something that I didn't feel? Would that do the trick? It was terribly difficult for me to confess a feeling I didn't have. I desperately wanted to be saved, but I also wanted to be honest.

Certain writers and speakers say that we human beings cannot comprehend the real meaning of the cross or appreciate what it meant to Jesus. They say we shall have to wait until eternity to learn. But these remarks, instead of bringing me comfort made me feel more disturbed. I had understood from the New Testament that the apostles, including Paul, had been profoundly moved in their human lifetime by something about the cross. Something phenomenal got hold of them. They were willing to suffer "the loss of all things," and instead of crying about it, were actually "content with weaknesses, insults, hardships, persecutions, and difficulties for Christ's sake." 2 Corinthians 12:10, TEV.

I knew no such willingness to suffer for Christ's sake, certainly not to the extent of taking *pleasure* in suffering for Him! The apostles had something I didn't have; and apparently I couldn't get it until I got to heaven. But the distressing point was that I probably wouldn't be able to get to heaven unless first of all I had the requisite experience! I was trapped in a hopeless circle.

Someone may want to interrupt me here and say, "Too bad I couldn't have been there to help you out. You didn't need to feel any particular sense of appreciation for the cross of Christ. Just accept Him as your Saviour as you would sign up for an insurance policy. You don't sense any gratitude or emotion when you sign on the dotted line. And yet you are 'covered' the moment you sign up. That's all there is to being saved."

I had thought of that. I knew that many people look at it that way. But their complacency seemed to me a far cry from the apostles' burning devotion to Christ. Paul actually "gloried" in bearing a cross of sacrifice like Jesus bore:

"Three times I was whipped by the Romans; and once I was stoned [with rocks, not drugs!]. I have been in three shipwrecks, and once I spent twenty-four hours in the water. In my many travels I have been in danger from floods and from robbers, in danger from fellow Jews and from Gentiles; there have been dangers in the cities, dangers in the wilds, dangers on the high seas, and dangers from false friends. There has been work and toil; often I have gone without sleep; I have been hungry and thirsty; I have often been without enough food, shelter, or clothing.... If I must boast, I will boast about things that show how weak I am." 2 Corinthians 11:25-30, TEV.

The "insurance policy" kind of faith had barely enough power to drag its adherents out to sit on cushioned pews in church once a week. Jesus said, "None of you can be My disciple unless he gives up everything he has." "Whoever does not carry his own cross and come after Me cannot be My disciple." Luke 14:33, 27, TEV. That deeply impressed me. Either one finds the power to serve Christ as those apostles did, or he isn't a real Christian.

Those misgivings I had were right, and the fact that I had them was probably evidence the Holy Spirit had not forsaken me. Being a sinner, I was no better than anybody else; but neither was I worse than others. I had the *potential* for a true heart appreciation of Christ's cross. *What I lacked was an understanding of what was involved in the cross, what it meant to Him.*

My parents and pastors had ignorantly taught me an error that obscured the love of Christ and hid from me the full extent of its beauty and power. This error obscured the cross as heavy smog obscures one's view of snow-capped mountains. The apostles in the New Testament had been seeing something I had never seen, and what they saw moved them to their astounding heart devotion to Christ. I was spiritually paralyzed because I couldn't see what they saw.

WHAT HIDES THE CROSS FROM VIEW.

This error was the common idea of the natural immortality of the soul, the teaching that one cannot really die, that what we call death is merely an immediate release to another level of life. As a host of physical ills can result from a simple vitamin deficiency, so this basic error borrowed from ancient paganism but handed down through Christendom triggered a chain reaction of confusion in my understanding.

In the Garden of Eden the Creator had plainly told Adam and Eve that if they should sin, "in the day" of their transgression "you shall surely die." Genesis 2:17. He said exactly what He meant. It was the devil who flatly contradicted Him, telling them: "You will *not* surely die." Genesis 3:5.

In effect, the tempter was voicing the tenets of paganism and of much so-called Christianity when he said that there is no such thing as death itself. No man can utterly perish. The soul possesses a natural immortality.

This idea became not only the cornerstone of pagan religion, but from thence it infiltrated the doctrine of many Christian churches. The error may seem innocent enough at first thought; but consider what it does to our understanding of the cross of Christ:

■ It effectively contradicts the Scriptural statements, "Christ *died* for the ungodly," and "Christ died for us." Romans 5:6, 8.

■ In other words, the way Satan wants us to understand it, Christ didn't really die for us at all. He merely endured physical pain in which He was sustained throughout by the assurance that He had nothing to risk, nothing to lose, since He could not really die. If He had nothing to lose, He therefore had nothing to give of any value beyond the endurance of physical pain.

■ As soon as He cried out, "It is finished," He went to heaven. (Some say He went to "hell" in order to preach to the "spirits in prison;" but I reasoned that if He did, He went as a visiting missionary and not as one suffering the expected torments of the lost. Either way one looks at it, He didn't really die at all. He merely entered into a larger existence.)

Where is the sacrifice? Gone! And that helpless vanity is precisely what Satan wanted me to feel regarding the cross of Christ.

In comparison with the sufferings of martyrs or soldiers who die for their country, or heroes who die for their friends, there was nothing very special about what Jesus did. In fact, His sacrifice lacked one quality of nobility inherent in the self-sacrifice of soldiers and heroes: through it all He held fast to His own security, whereas they sacrifice *their* security. Jesus didn't really give up anything, least of all Himself. And when John 3:16 says that "God so loved the world that He *gave* His only begotten Son," it really means that the Father only *lent* Him.

This error of the natural immortality of the soul is intended by its author to cast a suspicion of make-believe into the story of Calvary— just enough to paralyze the devotion of those who profess to follow Christ. If their appreciation of Jesus' cross is beclouded, their love will be stifled, and their devotion hobbled.

THE REAL MEASURE OF JESUS' SACRIFICE.

The sufferings of Jesus were incomparably greater than the endurance of physical pain, or the torture of any of the martyrs. There was no sham or make-believe about the burden He bore. Scripture says, "The Lord has laid on Him the iniquity of us all." Isaiah 53:6.

What is "iniquity"? "Your iniquities have separated you from your God, and your sins have hidden His face from you." Isaiah 59:2. Iniquity leaves the soul desperately bereft and alone, destroys all sense of security. The Lord did indeed lay upon Christ "the iniquity of us all." This means that He laid upon Him the same feelings of guilt, loneliness, insecurity, and despair that we know so well. It was this burden laid upon Him that separated Christ from His Father.

Before I learned the truth, it had seemed that Christ could not possibly have really felt forsaken. The Bible says He cried out, "My God,

My God, why have You forsaken Me?" Was this a dramatic actor following a teleprompter, wailing his lines on the stage, or was this an honest cry from a heart wrung with bitter anguish?

Christ did not bear this burden as a man might carry a heavy load on his shoulders. He bore the burden deep within His own soul. Peter says, "Himself bore our sins *in His own body* on the tree." 1 Peter 2:24. It was therefore within His own nervous system, in His mind and soul, in His most inner consciousness that Jesus bore the killing load. Paul is even more explicit: "He [the Father] made Him who knew no sin 'o be sin for us." 2 Corinthians 5:21.

CHRIST WAS NOT A SINNER, FOR HE WAS SINLESS.

But He was made "a curse for us (for it is written, 'Cursed is everyone who hangs on a tree')." Galatians 3:13. The "sin" and the "curse" are here identical. Paul's statements indicate that Christ's identity with sin as He bore His cross was something terrifyingly real. "The wages of sin is death." Romans 6:23. If Christ was "made to be sin," "made a curse for us," it is clear that He was likewise made to suffer the wages of sin.

Christ is very close to us, "for both He [the sinless Christ] who sanctifies and those who are being sanctified [sinners] are all of one, for which reason He is not ashamed to call them brethren." Hebrews 2:11. But how did He bear our death?

WHAT IS DEATH, THOSE "WAGES OF SIN" WHICH CHRIST SUFFERED?

There are two kinds of death in Scripture: (a) one called sleep (see John 11:11, 13), which is the "death" we commonly speak of; and (b) the other is the real thing, the second death (see Revelation 2:11; 20:6; 21:8). The latter is eternal separation from God—good-bye to light, joy, and life, forever.

It was this "second death" that Jesus experienced. "He, by the grace of God, might taste death for everyone." Hebrews 2:9. Since He tasted it for everyone, this sleep that we call death cannot be what He "tasted," because everyone tastes that kind of death for himself. Whatever it was that Jesus tasted, it was that we might not have to taste it ourselves.

Christ in fact died the death that the Creator promised Adam and Eve that they should die if they sinned, the death that sin will bring to the lost at last. Jesus felt it as much as any human being can feel it, because "in all things He had to be made like His brethren.... He Himself has suffered, being tempted." Verses 17, 18. Therefore the death that Jesus died on the cross was the full bitter cup of despair and ruin that will be the eventual "wages of sin."

This had to involve the hiding of His Father's face. There is no hope, no light, in the second death, neither is there expectation of a resurrection to brighten its despair. No candle light even at the end of the tunnel. If Jesus "died for our sins" or "died for us" (1 Corinthians 15:3; Romans 5:8), then He experienced in His final suffering a darkness that veiled from His sight the expectation of a resurrection. If He had been buoyed up by the hope of resurrection, to that extent He would have come short of "tasting death for everyone" or truly *giving* Himself "for our sins." At best He could only have *lent* Himself, which would not be *giving* Himself.

No wonder Christ's human nature recoiled against that terrifying experience! He flung Himself on the ground in Gethsemane: "My soul is exceeding sorrowful, even unto death," He groaned. "He went a little farther and fell on His face, and prayed, saying, 'O My Father, if it is possible, let this cup pass from Me; nevertheless not as I will, but as You will.'" Matthew 26:38, 39.

The cup which He drank was something no other human being before or since has ever fully tasted. In fact, since time began, He is the one and only person ever to have *truly* died. The full terror of hopelessness in the second death is what He "tasted" in the full consciousness of its for-eternity killing reality. Neither the nails driven through His hands and feet nor the floggings killed Him. He scarcely felt the physical pain on the cross, so terrible was the intense soul suffering that evoked a perspiration of blood in Gethsemane and at last literally broke His heart. "Reproach has broken My heart, and I am full of heaviness." Psalm 69:20.

Throughout His life and even through some hours of His final passion, Jesus knew a bright confidence in His resurrection. He lived as in the very sight of His Father's smiling face. In that divine sunshine no shadows could terrify Him. Even when the repentant thief pleaded, "Remember me," Jesus still retained His joyful confidence, for He promised, Assuredly I say to you today, you will be with Me in Paradise. Luke 23:43. (There is no comma in the original.)

But not yet had Christ drained the cup to its bitter dregs. There was to come a change.

THE THREAT OF ETERNAL FAILURE IN HIS MISSION.

To press that bitter cup deeply to the Savior's lips, the wicked tempter used as his agency the people Christ had come to save.

While on the cross, Jesus could not help hearing the people say to each other, "*If* He is the King of Israel, let Him now come down from the cross, and we will believe Him. He trusted in God; let Him deliver Him now if He will have Him: for He said, 'I am the Son of God.'" Some challenged Him directly, "*If* You are the Son of God, come down from the cross." Matthew 27:42, 43, 40.

We have no right to think that Jesus was unaffected by these taunts. That tempting *if* was terrible to bear in His hour of extreme humiliation. "Let God deliver Him now, *if* He will have Him!" His hands nailed to the bars, Jesus had no way to shut His ears to their taunts and insinuations. All He could do was pray. But it seemed that no one in heaven would listen to Him. "You do not hear," He complained. Psalm 22:2.

For hours He wrestled with the awful burden. Some time after those malicious *ifs* "from the sixth hour until the ninth hour there was darkness over all the land" (three o'clock in the afternoon), when Jesus "cried out with a loud voice" those words of forsaken loneliness that indicated He now felt the terror of entire separation from His Father. Matthew 27:45, 46.

Like a barbed arrow tipped with poison, that last temptation of despair caused Him His most bitter anguish.

Darkness mercifully veiled His agony when He was unable to use His crucified hands to hide His tear-stained face from the gaze of the mocking crowds. Only His broken, sobbing voice could be heard in the pitch blackness that enveloped Calvary. How cruel humans can be! And how merciful was the Father to wrap His tortured Son in folds of darkness while He suffered so! No angel even was allowed to see the sight of His anguished human face as He uttered those despairing words, nor was Christ permitted to feel the kiss of love and loyalty the Father longed to press upon Him in the gloom. The Father was there with Him, suffering with Him, for "God was in Christ reconciling the world to Himself." 2 Corinthians 5:19. But Christ must be left to *feel* forsaken, to "tread the winepress alone," fearfully so.

SOMETHING IN HIM HELD ON; SOMETHING HE WILL SHARE WITH US.

But although hope died, love endured. There is a strange psalm that describes the horrible experience that Christ went through. It opens a window for us that we might peer into Christ's heart as He hangs on the cross in the long hours of darkness.

He hears the taunts of the people and ponders the mysterious silence of His Father. Psalm 22 tells how He recalls that His ancestors got answers when *they* prayed. Why couldn't He? "*They* trusted, and You delivered *them. They* cried to You, and were delivered: *they* trusted in You, and were not ashamed. But *I* am a worm, and no man; a reproach of men, and despised of the people." "*I* cry in the daytime, but You do not hear." Verses 4-6, 2.

That's a terrible way for anyone to feel! When you feel that *no one* cares, not even God, despair is distilled into its final death-dealing poison. The truth is that no other human soul has ever had to drink that same cup of pure despair mingled with the guilt of the whole world's sin laid upon His consciousness. Christ is "the true Light which gives light to every man coming into the world" (John 1:9) and sustains everyone in his/her darkest hours with a clear-shining ray of hope. The Holy Spirit presses upon our souls the assurance, *"Somebody cares!"* Even if you've spent your life in wrong-doing, you can see some hope in those last moments.

But Jesus must see no such hope, feel no such assurance. "I have trodden the winepress *alone*," He says. Isaiah 63:3. He drinks the cup to its bitterest dregs.

Nevertheless, He must find some way to bridge the dark gulf between His forsaken soul and the Father. He must overcome this conviction of separation. He must achieve an atonement, a reconciliation with Him. If the Father forsakes Him, He will not forsake His Father! If He can see no bridge over the dark chasm of ultimate human and divine despair, as the Son of God, the Crown Prince of glory, He will build one!

The inspired psalm tells what happened. Christ's mind goes back to His human infancy in Bethlehem. Though *now* "You do not hear," yet "You are He who took Me out of the womb: You made Me trust when I was on My mother's breasts. I was cast upon You from birth, from My mother's womb." Tortured in spirit, He relies on the events in His life that prove the Father's care for Him. If God heard the prayers of "our fathers" and if He protected Me, the infant Jesus in those born-in-a-stable days in Bethlehem, surely He will not turn away now!

Christ understands His mercy and great love; surely He will not fail Me now! "By faith" the anguished Son of God will bridge the chasm—as a human being *He will believe His Father's love in the darkness and in the torments of hell.*

As the final moment of endurance comes, He feels like one being tossed on the horns of savage beasts: "Save Me from the lion's mouth and from the horns of the wild oxen [wild African buffalo]!" Psalm 22:21. In that last desperate moment His faith breaks through the impenetrable darkness, and He triumphs. Like Jacob wrestling with the Angel in the darkness, Christ grasps the Father who is not permitted to embrace Him, and He clings to Him by faith: *"You have heard Me!"* The Father may forsake Him, but He will not forsake the Father! The new Jacob cries out, "I will not let You go unless you bless Me!" Christ's faith endures, even through the horrors of the "second death."

"HEREIN IS LOVE."

When once the error had been cleared away, I began to see the cross as it is. I began "to understand how broad and long, how high and deep, is Christ's love.... although it can never be fully known." Ephesians 3:18, 19, TEV. The picture that had been so foggy, now was in sharper focus. At last I was in the kindergarten.

Here at last I began to see the love that moved the apostles so wonderfully. No longer did their self-sacrificing devotion appear so phenomenal or impossible. The love they knew appears more and more to be the normal, proper response of any honest human heart to the sacrifice Christ made. Yes, "in the cross of Christ I glory."

But still a gulf in understanding remains that tends to separate us from that full fellowship with Christ that the apostles knew. Let us now search for the truth that by faith spans that chasm.

Chapter 10

HOW THE CROSS CASTS OUT OUR HUMAN FEAR

CREATURES THAT GOD HAS MADE DON'T FIND IT HARD TO BE THEMSELVES. We marvel at the strength of the lion, the grace of the gazelle, the flight of the eagle, but do not praise them for their respective feats because they are just doing what they were made to do.

The eagle knows within himself no conflict between the desire to be an earthbound creature and the urge to be an eagle. He is satisfied to be what he was made to be. We humans likewise find it comparatively easy to do what we were gifted to do, and impossible to do what we feel we were not gifted to do.

One often wonders if it wasn't easy for Jesus to bear His cross. Wasn't He the Son of God? As such wasn't it natural and easy for Him to do His Father's will?

If so, His sacrifice has little meaning for us, because we most definitely do not find it easy to do what is right, and certainly not to bear a cross. As well might an eagle tell an earth-bound animal, "Follow me," as for Christ to tell *me* to take up my cross and follow Him!

Any poor animal would be frustrated trying to soar over the clouds, whereas the eagle would find it the easiest thing he has ever done. Yes, Christ is the Son of God who "delights" to do His Father's will. We are often tempted to think it seems a piece of effrontery for Him to tell us,

"Take My yoke upon you.... For My yoke is easy and My burden is light." Matthew 11:29, 30. We are as much different from Him, we suppose, as a horse is different from an eagle. What is easy to the eagle is impossible to a different creature.

This problem troubled me for years until I discovered a truth in the Gospels that seemed like the opening of another window into the depths of the heart of Christ.

DID CHRIST HAVE AN INWARD STRUGGLE?

If He found it easy to bear His cross and follow His Father's will, He must have had only one will, that is, the will of His Father, as an eagle has only one will, that is, the will to be what he was created to be. The eagle knows no conflict wishing to be something else than a flying bird.

A certain prophecy had led me to think Jesus had only one will. Speaking prophetically of Christ, the psalm records His own words: "Then I said, 'Behold, I come; in the scroll of the book it is written of me. I *delight* to do Your will, O my God, and Your law is within my heart.'" Psalm 40:7, 8. So important is this matter of Jesus' "will" that the writer of the book of Hebrews adds that it is "by that will we have been sanctified through the offering of the body of Jesus Christ once for all." Hebrews 10:10. The "will of Jesus" is page one news in Bible teaching.

Now it began to look to me as though Jesus was a kind of automaton, a human machine that "delighted" in doing what everybody else in the world, or at least I and most people I knew, found it impossible to do. There was my "Eagle," flying in the clouds and enjoying it, while I stumbled around below saying to myself, "He says, 'Follow Me'; but I can't!"

BUT I HAD NOT READ FAR ENOUGH.

When Jesus came, Scripture says that the Father sent Him "in the likeness of sinful flesh, on account of sin: He condemned sin *in* the flesh." Romans 8:3. Evidently the "Eagle" became what I am, an earthbound creature, gave up His wings! If Christ came "in the likeness of sinful flesh," that is, *my* flesh, He must have had as much of a conflict in that flesh as I do in mine; and it would have been no more easy for Him to do His Father's will than it is for me. It was in *my* human flesh that He "condemned sin," not in sinless flesh. It would be pretty silly for an eagle to condemn a cow for not being able to fly. The animal could well retort, "What do *you* know about my real condition?"

I found that Jesus acknowledged openly that He had as much of a conflict in His soul as I have in mine. True, He was infinitely different than I am because He never gave in to a selfish will whereas I have. But as Son of man, He faced the problem of two wills; and it was not without a terrible struggle that He surrendered His own will to follow His Father's will.

Although the psalm said of Him, "I delight to do My Father's will," note what it cost Him: "My soul is exceeding sorrowful, even to death.... O My Father, if it is possible, let this cup pass from Me; nevertheless, not as I will, but as You will." Matthew 26:38, 39. Here was a frightful conflict.

Jesus had a will of His own that was naturally opposed to bearing the cross, just as I have a will of my own that is likewise opposed. He said openly, "*Not* as I will." What He did is as clear as sunlight: He denied His own will. Further, it is plain that it was impossible for Him to follow His Father's will unless He first denied His own will, because the two wills were in direct conflict. *They formed a cross.*

Awesome thought!

TALK ABOUT CONFLICT!

I began to feel ashamed of myself for ever imagining that Jesus had none.

But then, I thought, conflict means different things to different people. Some love it because they find it easy. This denying His own will that Jesus did—perhaps it was easy for Him. I found it hard to deny my own will, but perhaps I was mistakenly projecting onto Jesus my own experience.

Then I remembered what Luke says about Jesus' struggle: "And being in *agony*, He prayed more earnestly. Then his sweat became like great drops of blood falling down to the ground." Luke 22:44. 1 then felt even more ashamed of myself for imagining that the conflict was easy for Him!

NOT ONLY IN GETHSEMANE DO WE FIND RECORD OF HIS STRUGGLE.

It had continued all through His life. "I can of Myself do nothing: … I do not seek My own will *but* the will of the Father who sent Me." John 5:30. "I have come down from heaven, *not* to do My own will, *but* the will of Him who sent Me." John 6:38. In other words, He came down from heaven to fight our battle in our place, with our flesh and nature, to endure the conflict we must endure, and to surrender His will where we have sinfully, selfishly, followed our will.

His "follow Me" therefore makes sense because He "condemned sin" (that is, self-will) in *our* flesh. Never did it get the upper hand for a moment; but the struggle was terrible, far more severe than our own. And in so doing He made a profound difference in human living on this planet.

I was completely wrong when I thought that Christ was a kind of automaton. He was a free man, left to choose for Himself which way He would choose to go. In fact, love cannot exist without freedom. A doll may have a tape recorder in it which says, "I love you," but no one cares what it says.

But still another problem arose. Wasn't Christ a kind of spiritual "genius"? His love was wonderful—no question. And His voluntary surrender of Himself throughout life and at the cross is amazing. But still the question persisted, "Isn't it about as impossible for me to follow Christ's way as it is to follow the mathematical genius of an Einstein?" I never was very good at mathematics in school. If God told me that in order for me to get to heaven, *I* must also invent the mathematics for an atom bomb as Einstein did, I'd throw up my hands in despair, although I might wish very much I could do it.

I can marvel at what Einstein did, and I can also marvel at what Christ did. But there my following seems to end.

BUT I DISCOVERED ONE IMPORTANT DIFFERENCE.

Einstein's genius for math was not like Christ's genius for love. Einstein never offered to teach me anything, never made any promise that if I could follow him, "Look to me, and you'll be inventing all kinds of nuclear marvels." (This illustration of the atom bomb is something completely backward to what I want to say. If you can imagine something the exact opposite, something fully as powerful but fraught with corresponding good for the world, you'll have what I want. Think of a dynamic love that turns our modem world upside down and reverses all the human selfishness that plagues us—that's it.)

But Christ did promise me that I could receive in my heart the same love He had! He would teach me His "genius" for it so that I could become, not a little Einstein working scientific wizardry, but something infinitely more wonderful—a "representative" of Christ serving in His loving ministry to my fellowmen.

Not that Christ ever promised me that I could really *duplicate* Him, but the world would at least imagine I did. I could be close to Him in unselfish service. That is what they thought of the disciples at Antioch when they called them (for the first time) "Christians" (which meant—like Christ, close to Him).

AND THEN I FOUND THE SCRIPTURE THAT BRIDGED THE LAST GAP.

Philippians 2:5-8 (RSV) spoke of the steps of sacrifice Christ took in leaving His exalted place in heaven, seven of them:

(1) Counting His equality with God nothing to be "grasped."

(2) "Emptying Himself."

(3) Taking upon Him the "form of a servant" (slave, in the Greek).

(4) Stepping lower than angels (who are all servants) in that He was made "in the likeness of men."

(5) Choosing to be born not as a king in a royal palace or as a child of wealth, but "being found in appearance as a man, … humbled Himself" (NKJV), and accepted the rude, toilsome life of a peasant, working with His hands for a living.

(6) Becoming at the end "obedient unto death."

That last step made me pause. As I thought about it, I began to realize that no suicide is "obedient unto death." What he/she wants is sleep and unconsciousness, not the terror of the second death. *But Christ was obedient unto the curse of being hanged on the tree.* Galatians 3:13. It was "tasting" eternal condemnation, drinking, in an infinite sense, the poison of that soul-destroying "curse," salivating it, absorbing it, for "everyone." Infinite bitterness! As our God-man, He could endure human pain and agony to an infinite degree, a degree that no human has ever been able to "taste."

But then what bridged the gap for me was the command which preceded this recital of Christ's sacrifice: "*Let* this [same] mind be in you." Philippians 2:5. We can never repeat His sacrifice, but we can learn to appreciate it.

In other words, if I would just *let* the Holy Spirit write that mind of Christ in me, His will would become my will just as His Father's will became His will for Him. Thereafter, to put it in simple words, what Jesus was to His neighbors I would be to mine. And moreover, I would "delight" in it. No more moaning about what great sacrifices I was making.

But there was that last step:

(7) As we have seen, that "death of the cross" involved for Jesus the surrender of His eternal security.

It is encouraging that such self-emptying love *is* a possibility for sinful man through Christ. Christ *can* dwell in human hearts by faith, and we *can* learn to serve Him from love and not from selfish motives. But has anyone ever done so?

THERE WERE TWO PEOPLE WHO KNEW SOMETHING OF THAT LOVE.
■ One was Moses. Israel had "committed a great sin" in that they

had made and worshipped a golden calf. The Lord proposed to Moses that he step aside. "Let Me alone," He said, "that I may destroy them and blot out their name from under heaven; and I will make of you a nation mightier and greater than they." Deuteronomy 9:14. To take the place of Abraham, Isaac, and Jacob as the progenitor of the "chosen people"! What a great honor! This proposal would guarantee Moses' salvation and his everlasting honor.

Naturally it was a severe temptation to him. So far as Israel was concerned, he could reason that he had no obligation toward them, for they had sinned and deserved to perish. But Moses did something totally contrary to our natural human nature.

He proposed that someone else's name be blotted out from under heaven—his own, if Israel could not be forgiven: "If You will forgive their sin—but if not, I pray, blot me out of Your book which You have written." Exodus 32:32. Moses' love was stronger than his desire for personal security in heaven, or for eternal life and honor. Can you imagine?

■ Another man who knew that same self-emptying love was Paul: "I could wish that I myself were accursed from Christ for my brethren, my countrymen [relatives] according to the flesh, who are Israelites." Romans 9:3, 4.

So long as our predominant motive for following Christ is our own desire for personal security, we will fail of receiving the "mind of Christ" and thus come short of bearing the cross. Christ was no "opportunist;" neither was Moses or Paul. Neither are His people who "follow the Lamb wherever He goes."

THE "OLD MAN" HAS ONE LAST STAND HE TAKES.

The last bastion he holds is covetousness of reward and its natural bulwark—fear of personal loss. It is of course severely anti-cross.

There was present in the first sin of man a desire for equality with God, to be as God, to possess natural immortality. Our first parents knew no fear until they cherished that desire. That same fear will underlie the last sin of man; and the cross is the only way to exchange it for love.

But what we call love is not love if fear is its foundation. Self-interest is not the basis of genuine love, which is *agape*. The search for one's own security is the reverse of genuine love. This is evident from what John says, "There is no fear in love [*agape*]; but perfect love [*agape*] casts out fear, because fear involves torment. But he who fears has not been made perfect in love." 1 John 4:18.

John is discussing our basic problem of anxiety. We are all born with it. Its "torment" is expressed in many ways, including diseases of the body that have their source in this underlying bedrock of anxiety. Holistic medicine recognizes that migraine headaches, colitis, ulcers, asthma, and many other diseases can have their source here.

When Christ, "the Sun of Righteousness," arises in the heart, there is "healing in His wings." Malachi 4:2. The healing comes with the casting out of fear and anxiety.

But how is fear "cast out"?

Through the crucifixion of the "old man," the self who is "crucified with Christ." Anxiety is the fear in which the self is nourished. Although fear is something open that we can see, like a railroad train bearing down upon us, anxiety is a fear that is beneath the surface, a dread we cannot tangibly recognize and identify in the open, because the real identity of the "old man" is never full and complete.

How does love cast out fear?

Seeing the love of Christ revealed at the cross does it.

We have seen that the bridge that spans the last chasm between us and full fellowship with Christ is the surrender of the will in precisely the same way that Christ, in our flesh, surrendered His will. "By that will [God's] we have been sanctified through the offering of the body of Jesus Christ once for all."

Therefore we have "boldness to enter the Holiest by the blood of Jesus, by a new and living way which He consecrated for us, through the veil, that is, His flesh." Hebrews 10:10, 19, 20. As He surrendered His will to the Father, He fulfilled that love. As we surrender our will to Him, that same love is forthwith fulfilled in us. The way to boldness is through His flesh.

Anxiety is basically what the Bible calls the "fear of death." What we have called "death" the Bible calls "sleep." Few fear that. Our "fear of death" is that of the *second* death, a fear of the nakedness, aloneness, forsakenness, the horror of great darkness, that comes when one is forever separated from the life and light of God and His great universe of joy.

This buried anxiety touches every aspect of our waking life and even intrudes upon us in our dreams. We have seen that only as we sense the dimensions of Christ's sacrifice on the cross can we possibly come to grips with that problem of naked anxiety.

YOU ARE CAPABLE OF RESPONDING TO CHRIST'S LOVE.

If someone gave you a precious gift, your most natural response would be to say a fervent thank you. And, further, according to the value of the gift, your most natural response would be a desire to demonstrate your gratitude to the friend for what he did. This capacity for glad, thankful response is built into your human nature, a part of the package that is you. It is almost instinctive. Dozens of times a day we will catch ourselves saying thank you for kindnesses done, and as often will we find ourselves watching for opportunities to respond.

This simple, unaffected, uncomplicated response of our humanity is all that God has ever asked from anyone. Christ *gave* Himself for us on the cross. If we don't see it, or can't sense how there was any real gift or sacrifice involved, there will naturally be no response of loving sacrifice on our part, only the self-centered desire for our own personal security which leaves fear still intact. Such a halfhearted, lukewarm response is inevitable from anyone's heart when Satan succeeds in obscuring the reality of what Christ gave for us.

But when we see what happened at Calvary, something does begin to move us. "Through death [the second death]" Christ destroyed "him who had the power of death, that is, the devil, and" thus released "those who through fear of death were all their lifetime subject to bondage." Hebrews 2:14, 15. Truly,

> None of the ransomed ever knew
> How deep were the waters crossed,
> Nor how dark was the night that the Lord passed through
> Ere He found His sheep that was lost.

BUT WE DO KNOW A *LITTLE* SOMETHING ABOUT IT!

Our search is begun. As Satan seeks more and more to ensnare us in the allurements of self-seeking, sensual or material, we shall find something wonderful happening. As "sin abounds," the stronger grace of Christ will "much more abound." As we remember the cross, Satan will be defeated continually. Many people all around the world will respond exactly as Paul did:

"We are *ruled* by the love of Christ, now that we recognize that one Man died for everyone, which means that they all share in His death. He died for all, so that those who live should no longer live for themselves, but only for Him who died and was raised to life for their sake." 2 Corinthians 5:14, 15, TEV.

It simply becomes almost impossible for anyone who sees it to live any longer unto himself! Talk about power. This must be what Paul meant when he said, "The message of the cross ... is the power of God." 1 Corinthians 1:18.

Power for what? To change that most changeless thing—a self-centered human mind. The old patterns of thought are changed, and love *rules*.

I hope no one will misunderstand me as I say this, it actually becomes easy to follow Christ! Jesus promised that it would be when He said, "My yoke is easy and My burden is light." Matthew 11:30. The cross supplies the missing element.

Now we can see what Paul meant when he said, "God forbid that I should glory, except in the cross of our Lord Jesus Christ." And now that we, too, have had a glimpse of what he saw in his day, our hearts cry out with all our being, "Yes, Paul, we're with you! We kneel, too, at the feet of the Crucified One and confess Him Lord of our lives, King of our love, eternal Sovereign of our hearts."

> Where'er I go, I'll tell the story
>> Of the cross;
> In nothing else my soul shall glory,
>> Save the cross.
> And this my constant theme shall be,
> Through time and in eternity,
> That Jesus tasted death for me
>> On the cross.
>
>   ↫ Anon.

Chapter 11

MARY MAGDALENE AND THE CROSS

↶

WHAT CAN THE TRUTH OF THE CROSS DO FOR ONE WHOSE LIFE HAS BEEN A TRAGIC MESS? Here's a basket-case woman so badly twisted out of shape that the Bible says "seven devils" had control of her. Mark 16:9.

"And being in Bethany at the house of Simon the leper, as He sat at the table, a woman came having an alabaster flask of very costly oil of spikenard. Then she broke the flask and poured it on His head.

"But there were some who were indignant among themselves,[1] and said, 'Why was this fragrant oil wasted? For it might have been sold for more than three hundred denarii[2] and given to the poor.' And they criticized her sharply.

"But Jesus said, 'Let her alone. Why do you trouble her? She has done a good work for Me. For you have the poor with you always, and whenever you wish you may do them good; but Me you do not have always.

"'She has done what she could. She has come beforehand to anoint My body for burial. Assuredly, I say to you, wherever this gospel is preached in the whole world, what this woman has done will also be told as a memorial to her.'" Mark 14:3-9.

When Mary broke the alabaster flask of precious ointment to anoint Jesus, she was giving to the world her unconscious expression of that same spirit of love and sacrifice which Jesus' life and death exemplified. Thus Mary's act has special meaning for us as an illustration of the truth of the cross.

This poignant act at Bethany is the most beautiful, heart-touching deed ever performed by a repentant sinner.[3] It was welcome evidence to Jesus and to the watching universe that humanity is indeed capable of attaining a profound heart appreciation of the sacrifice Jesus made. Mary had no righteousness of her own; but her Savior's righteousness had been truly imparted to her.

Imagine how her noble deed cheered the heart of the Savior in His darkest hours! No mighty angel from heaven could have brought to Him the comfort which the memory of her tearful sacrifice imparted; for in her sacrificial love to Him He discerned a pledge of His eventual joy. The travail of His soul will purchase for Him a precious reward—the making of many righteous through "faith which works through love." Galatians 5:6.

The evoking of such repentant love in human hearts changes lives. Surely this is the end to be achieved by the Savior's sacrifice!

A DEBT TO CHRIST, AND A DEBT TO THIS WOMAN!

The world may owe something to Mary which it has never recognized for thus encouraging the sorely tempted One in His time of greatest need. Surely the cold-hearted Twelve gave Him no such comfort as did Mary, whom they despised!

But Mary knew not why she had been moved to make this strange, prodigal offering. Informed only by the inscrutable yet infallible reason of love, she had spent her all to buy this extravagant ointment. What really happened was that she anointed beforehand Christ's body for the burial.

She was so completely unable to defend her action before the reproachful disciples that Jesus Himself had to come to her rescue. In undertaking her defense before the unfeeling obtuseness of the Twelve, He transformed the incident into a lesson on the meaning of the cross— something the church of today hungers to understand.

In fact, from what He said, a sympathetic appreciation of Mary's mysterious deed is necessary if we would understand the gospel itself. Jesus bespoke for her act the high regard of His followers in all ages: "Wherever this gospel is preached throughout the whole world, what this woman did will also be spoken of as a memorial to her." Infinitely better than any marble inscription for a Roman emperor!

Here is reason enough for giving Mary our attention.

WHY DID JESUS PRAISE HER SO EXTRAVAGANTLY?

Not for her sake, but for the sake of "this gospel," the fragrance of her deed is to be published abroad like this. Here is the key to all that is perplexing in this strange event. *Mary was preaching a sermon.*

■ Her act illuminates the gospel and casts into sharp and grand relief its principles of love, sacrifice, and magnificence.

■ Likewise the faultfinding of the disciples exposes our natural human reaction to the tender love revealed at the cross.

■ Had we been present on the occasion, we would have found it difficult not to take our stand with Judas and the other disciples.

Mary had done something that was to all human appearance irrational and wasteful. "Three hundred denarii," the value of the ointment, represented the wages of a laboring man for a full year, "a denarius a day" being the usual pay. Matthew 20:2. Such a sum would probably have been sufficient to provide a small meal for five thousand men "besides women and children," according to Philip's cautious estimate. John 6:7; Matthew 14:21.

If we did not know the outcome of this drama of Bethany, what would we have thought of this apparently senseless extravagance? How many church managers and committee members would approve of such an expenditure? Who among us would not have sympathized decidedly with the disciples in their feelings of outrage? This emotionally disturbed woman deserves rebuke!

We would find our hearts ready to second Judas's motion of censure: "Why was not this fragrant oil sold for three hundred denarii and given to the poor?"

BUT JESUS HIMSELF STEPS IN TO DEFEND MARY.

According to our natural judgment, we would be ready to agree with Judas. Would it not be a more sober, practical act of devotion for Mary to use a few drops of the precious ointment to anoint His head, and then sell the balance for the benefit of the poor? We might feel a vague sense of thankfulness that such zealots as Mary are only a small minority in the church today.

But even more perplexing is the apparently reckless extravagance with which Jesus defended her. We are inclined to think He might have said something nice to her, tenderly commending the warmth of her affection while gently deploring this wild extravagance of its expression. He could have kindly encouraged her and at the same time placated the indignation of the Twelve.

Not so! While the hapless penitent tries to escape unnoticed, overwhelmed with confusion and embarrassment, fearing that her sister Martha and possibly even Jesus will think her foolish and improvident, Jesus lifts His voice above the murmuring of the disciples: "Let her alone. Why do you trouble her? She has done a good work for Me." Far from approving the disciples' apparent regard for the poor, He places an entirely different interpretation on Mary's motive. It was a far truer charity. Her deed was a parable of divine love, a vehicle for proclaiming the gospel. Jesus was forced to defend her, for in so doing He was defending Himself and His cross. He was, in fact, imparting to her deed a symbolic meaning of which she herself was ignorant.

■ In the alabaster bottle, broken at His feet, He discerned His body, broken and bruised for us.

- In the precious ointment running to waste on the floor, He saw His blood "shed for many for the remission of sins," yet rejected and despised by most of them.
- In the motive that prompted Mary's act—her heartbroken, repentant love for Him—Jesus saw the true reflection of His love for us.
- In her sacrifice to purchase the ointment with the sum total of her hard-earned savings, He saw the utter emptying of Himself in the role of the divine Lover of our souls.
- In her apparent extravagance He saw the magnificence of Heaven's offering poured out sufficient to save a world, yet accepted by only a handful of its inhabitants.

Thus was Jesus obliged to defend His wondrous cross before those who should have had hearts to appreciate its unutterable worth.

PATHETICALLY, WE SEE OURSELVES IN THE COLD-HEARTED SIMON AND THE TWELVE.

Judas had only sneers of contempt for the purest and holiest love eternity had known; and the slow-hearted, unappreciative disciples could only follow the promptings of his selfish criticism. Dare we think ourselves holier than they?

Hardly. We do well to remember that Mary was informed by the mysterious promptings of the Holy Spirit, an inspiration that stoops to give no reason. Only in a broken and a contrite heart can that inspiration find entrance.

The disciples were conscious of no such promptings, yet they had privately received clear teachings about Jesus' approaching death that Mary likely had not heard. They should have had preparatory understanding of the cross. But now an untaught woman with a penitent heart preached a *sermon* on the cross more eloquent even than Peter's at Pentecost, a sermon that to this day thrills the hearts of those who ponder its meaning. Thus we see that acquaintance with the historical details of the crucifixion is nothing compared with a heart appreciation of it. If flesh and blood cannot understand the doctrine of Christ's person, as the Savior said at Caesarea Philippi, neither can flesh and blood understand the doctrine of the cross.

MARY'S DEED ILLUSTRATES CHRIST'S SACRIFICE FOR US.

Consider the *motive* that prompted Mary. It was not for any hope of reward or even desire for praise that she did this unusual act. She had hoped to do it unnoticed. Only the sudden fragrance that filled the room betrayed her. Love alone was her guiding principle, love that in turn was a reflection of Jesus' love for sinners.

What was the motive that led Jesus to His cross? Theologians may write their ponderous tomes in efforts to account for the strange act at Calvary, only to return, weary at last, to the realization that no reason can be given: love alone was the motive.

How encouraging to Jesus to see reflected in Mary the image of His own character! In a sinner, do you ask? Yes, in "a woman … who *was* a sinner" (Luke 7:37) and a grievous one at that, He saw Himself reflected. As a positive print of a photograph from a negative, He saw in her love the print or likeness of His own pattern-love. "Reproach has broken My heart," He said (Psalm 69:20); repentance had now broken her heart through the ministry of His own broken heart

Wonder, O heavens, and be astonished, O earth, for the plan of salvation is a success! Whether the divine risk of Calvary is as yet seen to be justified so far as the cold-hearted Twelve are concerned, it is a success for the daughter of Bethany! The sacrifice of God in Christ has elicited from her soul its complementary sacrifice: "a broken spirit, a broken and a contrite heart," which God, fortunately different from the disciples, will "not despise." Psalm 51:17.

AGAIN, CONSIDER THE *SACRIFICE* OF MARY'S DEED.

It shines brightest when compared with the sacrifice of Jesus' offering Himself for us. In commending her, He said, "She has done what she could," the intent being that she had done *all* that she could. He too "has done what [He] could!" If Mary was ever rewarded in a temporal way for the almost endless days of humble toil expended for the purchase of the ointment, we do not know. But O that He who emptied Himself— "humbled Himself and became obedient to death, ... even the death of the cross" (Philippians 2:8)—might find ample reward for His sacrifice! Cannot we who have no alabaster flask of ointment to break upon His head at least find tears with which to wash those feet pierced for us? O Jesus, can You not find in us "seven devils" to cast out, that we might learn to love You as Mary did?

THE *MAGNIFICENCE* OF MARY'S DEED SHINES BRIGHTEST WHEN LIKENED TO THAT OF JESUS' SACRIFICE.

The disciples' reasoning was, Why not use a little ointment? Why this extravagance with something so precious? Look, it's running to waste on the floor! Three hundred silver coins gone down the drain! Just a few drops on His head would have been enough, Mary!

So we would have reasoned!

To this day the human heart, when uninformed by inspiration, is unable to appreciate the magnificence of Calvary's sacrifice.

■ Why give the divine life "a ransom for many" when only a few will respond?

■ Why pour out a Niagara of self-sacrificing love when all but a trickle seemingly runs to waste?

■ The sacrifice made was sufficient to redeem all of earth's billions of sinners; why pay such a price when the ultimate returns will be so meager?

■ Why should the divine Form be racked with grief and tears over "Jerusalems" that know not of and care not for the day of their visitation?

■ Why not restrict the love and its expression to the few who will respond to its appeal rather than pour out such an infinite waste that seems so useless? [4]

Thus did the disciples reason concerning Mary's magnificence; thus do many reason today concerning Him of whom her love was but a type.

To answer we can only say that love is never genuine unless it is prodigal—wasteful. Love never stints, never calculates. Mary's "very precious" alabaster flask of ointment was not bought at a bargain sale. She paid the full price for the finest that could be purchased with no grudging thought of saving anything. One can imagine her asking the shopkeeper for some ointment. Seeing in her only a poor peasant, he suggests a cheap preparation. "Have you nothing better?" she asks.

"Yes, I have a better quality, but it will cost you two hundred denarii."

"Do you have anything still better than this?" she persists.

"Yes, I have only the very finest and most expensive, but it will cost three hundred. You can't afford that, Mary. It's only for a king or emperor!"

"Let me have it," she replies. With her motive of love, she can do nothing less.

Could God, who is Himself love, do less than His utmost? He thought not of how to effect the salvation of the redeemed at the least possible cost to Himself. Heaven, the "ivory palaces," the devotion of a myriad of angels, the thrones of an infinite universe, life eternal, yes, the precious companionship of the Father, *all* Christ freely spent in the giving of Himself. An ocean of the water of life to be expended lavishly, and the only returns to be a few fragile earthen vessels filled with human tears of love! How infinitely precious must those "bottles" (Psalm 56:8) be to Him! "O Israel, hope in the Lord; for with the Lord there is mercy, and with Him is *abundant* redemption." Psalm 130:7.

Simon the leper's cold reaction to Mary's deed disturbs us.

The host had been a silent witness to Mary's act of devotion. He seemed not to be concerned as were the Twelve with its extravagance. Darker surmisings even than those were coursing through his soul, honest as he was.

He had not yet accepted Jesus as a Savior, though he had hoped that He might indeed prove Himself to be the Messiah. Having experienced the thrill of a miraculous healing, he had condescended now to invite the Galilean and His rude followers to this social occasion in order to express his gratitude. In so doing, he avoided giving Jesus even the honor of recognition as a social equal. He offered Him no kiss of welcome, no ointment for His head, not even water for His feet, the smallest elementary courtesy in the Middle East of that day.

Beholding the sublime spectacle of a repentant sinner wiping the tearstained feet of the world's Savior with her hair, Simon reasoned darkly within himself, "This Man, if He were a prophet, would know who and what manner of woman this is who is touching Him, for she is a sinner." Luke 7:39. How little does the self-righteous heart discern the credentials of divinity!

In the parable by which He sought to enlighten poor Simon, Jesus reveals the lesson of the glory of the cross that enlightens every honest heart that will pause long enough to survey the wondrous scene:

> "'There was a certain creditor who had two debtors. One owed five hundred denarii, and the other fifty. And when they had nothing with which to repay, he freely forgave them both. Tell Me, therefore, which of them will love him more?' Simon answered and said, 'I suppose the one whom he forgave more.' And He said to him, 'You have rightly judged.'" Luke 7:41-43.

Simon, having been the instrument in leading Mary into sin originally, was clearly the debtor owing "five hundred denarii," not fifty. By contrasting Simon's cold-hearted lovelessness with the warm devotion of Mary, Jesus tactfully revealed to his darkened mind and heart the truly astounding realization that Mary's repentant love should have been his if the one forgiven most should love most.

More than seven devils had been troubling Simon! He, the self-righteous one, was bothered with an eighth, the evil spirit of self-righteousness which hid the presence of the other seven. But the light even now shining from the cross illumined Simon's heart and disclosed to him the almost hopeless sinner that he was. Only the infinite pity of Jesus saved him from an ultimate ruin greater than Mary's had been. Simon could have also sung the hymn, "Jesus, Lover of my soul," as Mary could.

WHY DO SOME PEOPLE LOVE MUCH AND SOME LOVE LITTLE?

The parable of Jesus was not intended to show that different degrees of obligation should be felt by different sinners. Both Simon and Mary were infinitely and eternally in debt to the divine Creditor. Mary's love however was due to the simple fact that she *knew* she was a sinner and had been forgiven *much*. Simon had been forgiven little because he *felt* that he had sinned but little.

Will anyone in God's eternal kingdom go about feeling superior to others? "*I* never did anything bad like the common run of people! *I* came from a good family and grew up on the right side of the tracks! *My* friends weren't the ordinary drop-outs, living loosely, or using drugs. *I* was pretty good on my own, and all I needed was a slight push from Christ to get me into the kingdom!"

Wouldn't such words seem more appropriate coming from some whiner outside the gates of the city than from someone inside?

O for Mary's tender conscience! If Paul could call himself "the chief of sinners," can we do less? What light the doctrine of the cross may shed upon the unfeeling heart of Laodicea, the last of the great seven churches of all history! Lukewarm, self-righteous saints will trail behind the publicans and harlots who, like Mary, will repent. "Many that are first shall be last; and the last first."

¹ These "some" are identified not as the pagan Romans or Greeks who might have been present, nor as the unbelieving Jews, but as none other than Jesus' own disciples! And the instigator of their murmuring turns out to be none other than Judas Iscariot, the betrayer. So blinded were the Eleven! They could do nothing other than to say "amen" to his disloyal spirit. See Matthew 26:8; John 12:4, 5.

² A *denarius* was a Greek coin equivalent in value to a workingman's wage for a day. See Matthew 20:2. Three hundred would be about a year's wages.

³ How can one who disbelieves that Jesus of Nazareth is the Son of God explain the amazing fact that Jesus is the only man in world history who has had His feet washed with tears?

⁴ This reasoning is held by many Christians today who adhere to strict Calvinistic predeterminism. They feel that Christ died only for the elect.

Chapter 12

THE CROSS AND PERFECT CHRIST LIKENESS

⌐

*N*EVER DID JESUS OFFER WORDS OF PRAISE MORE IMPRESSIVE THAN HIS APPROVAL OF MARY'S ACT. "She has done what she could," He said, implying that she could not have done more. He could hardly have said, "Well done, you good and faithful servant!" any more enthusiastically.

Such praise of Mary sets her forth as the model Christian:

■ Her experience of repentant love was the perfect reflection of His sacrifice on the cross.

■ What a photographic print is to a photographic negative, her repentant love was to His own love for the world. How wonderful that Jesus found someone He could display as an example of what He died to accomplish!

■ It was Mary's understanding of the cross that enabled her to "come beforehand to anoint My body for burial," Jesus implied.

■ Her "good work" lay in her "discerning the Lord's body," the same work that the apostle Paul says is so vital to our own participation in the Lord's Supper. 1 Corinthians 11:29.

This means that it was Mary's discernment of the cross that caused Jesus to set her forth as the model of true Christian experience. "Wherever this gospel is preached in the whole world, what this woman has done will also be told of as a memorial to her."

When one begins to understand the cross, he begins to understand himself. Mary could never have "done what she could" had she not understood the truth about herself. She learned not to think of herself more highly than she ought to think. Willing to discover the worst about her case in order to find the Savior, she would not fight the conviction that she was possessed of "seven devils." She learned how offensive is sin when she heard Jesus seven times rebuke the demons that had controlled her heart and mind. The most deeply fallen transgressor became the noblest example of a Christlike Christian because she had come to see herself truly as the "chief of sinners." She could appreciate what it meant to be saved from hell, because she had been to hell.

ARE WE POSSESSED OF FEWER DEVILS THAN WAS MARY?

If so, we may cast the first stone of supercilious disdain at her repentance as being other than that of a model Christian. Respectable Christians often regard a repentance such as Mary's as the norm only for prostitutes, publicans, or criminals. A much more modest and restrained repentance befits those who have not committed great sins! They think they need only a fraction of the depth and scope of Mary's repentance!

On the surface it may indeed appear that Jesus recognizes a vast difference in the magnitude of repentance different people should feel. His illustration used in speaking to Simon contrasts the debt of fifty denarii owed by one debtor with the debt of five hundred owed by the other. Apparently some people need to repent only one-tenth as much as others!

But let us not miss the point of Jesus' little parable. He did not intend to teach that the two debtors should feel a different amount of gratitude. Both were unable to pay, and both were eternally and infinitely in debt. Both should therefore feel an infinite repentance. When the Bible says "all have sinned," it means that "all *alike* have sinned." Romans 3:23, NEB. The sin of sins is the taproot of sin—self-love, coldheartedness, unbelief. Only an insight into the meaning of the cross can disclose this exceeding sinfulness. We *all* are debtors owing "five hundred." Our difficulty is simply that, like Simon, we have not *realized* it. We think we have been forgiven only fifty. This is why we love so little and are lukewarm in our devotion.

Of all the problems God has had to deal with through the ages, none is so difficult as the lukewarmness of the last-day church of Laodicea. No more effective weapon could the dragon have invented to use in his last battle to overcome the last segment of Christ's church. See Revelation 12:17. Were not the ingenuity of love truly infinite, God Himself might well despair of winning such a battle. He much prefers a hot war to a lukewarm war!

But the resources of His love are sufficient to assure the victory. His elect will be delivered from even this almost overmastering temptation.

SOMEONE MAY ASK WHAT BASIS WE HAVE FOR BEING SO HOPEFUL.

It is the same story of Mary and Simon that provides the assurance. Hopeless as the case of Mary seemed, possessed as she bad been of seven devils, the case of Simon was even more difficult. He was a greater sinner than Mary ever was.* His blindness to his own need left him feeling smug, self-satisfied, and superior. How easily Christ might have done what we are so often inclined to do—abandon Simon to his own pitiful darkness.

But not so. As much as He labored to save Mary, so much more did He labor to rescue Simon from the grip of cold-hearted pride that so nearly sealed his eternal doom. Even greater than the miracle of casting seven devils out of Mary was His effective ministry for the proud socialite.

Simon now saw himself in a new light. He saw what he had done to Mary. Jesus could have crushed him with ridicule and condemnation,

---

* How do we know that Simon was the one who originally ruined Mary's life? This conviction, held by devout Bible students for centuries, is sustained by the import of Jesus' parable. Simon saw himself as owing the "five hundred" denarii.

but His kindness in showing him the truth won his heart. We can only assume that such divine love was not expended on him in vain.

O Miracle-worker of Bethany, come to us today!

MARY'S LOVE IS THE "PERFECT" CHRISTIAN EXPERIENCE.

Having seen that Mary's great repentance was truly normal, the model for all Christians, let us consider how the love which led to her repentance was itself that of the model Christian. The awakening of such love in the human heart is the great end Christ longed to achieve by His offering on Calvary. The cross satisfied all the legal demands of a broken law, but it also worked miracles on human souls.

Seldom has this glory of the cross been clearly discerned. All too often the usual concept of Calvary's sacrifice is that of a judicial maneuver exacted by divine vengeance, a penalty vicariously paid, an offering made to placate the offended anger of God or to satisfy cold divine justice. The cross is seen as a spiritual lightning arrester through which the thunderbolts of God's hot wrath against sinners fall harmlessly to the ground.

Thus God is looked upon as an aggrieved Judge whose desire for revenge is satisfied by the cruelties inflicted on His Son at Calvary. Through His "vicarious" suffering He can bring Himself to pardon those who avail themselves of the legal provisions of a strange transaction known as the atonement. Long words are used in trying to explain the intricacies of a legalistic procedure.

It's no wonder that the doctrine of the atonement, thus presented, leaves many untouched. Gratitude, contrition, and love are unawakened. Only a sense of personal security is achieved, much as one feels when he has signed a business insurance coverage against risk.

Such a concept can never inspire the magnificent love that moved Mary. At best, only a staid and modest lukewarm devotion is possible. All that is needed to reproduce Mary's intense devotion in every believer is for the full truth of the cross to shine into the darkened chambers of our hearts:

■ Mary is not a unique person: she represents the church.

- There is no difference between her human nature and ours.
- Given her understanding of the cross, we too will know the full dimensions of her gratitude and love.
- The gospel has lost none of its power. Liberated from the confusion of error, it will again accomplish in millions of human hearts the same glorious work accomplished in the heart of Mary.
- This promise is disclosed in the amazing prophecy in Revelation 18:1-4 of an angel coming down from heaven to lighten the earth with glory, and a heavenly voice penetrating to the inner consciousness of every human being, "Come out of [Babylon], My people."

BUT SUCH POWERFUL LOVE MUST CONTEND WITH THE OPPOSITION OF THE "SAINTS."

The drama of Bethany illustrates the conflict of all ages. In despising Mary's love, the disciples were joining with the world in despising enthusiasm in the service of Christ. Had Jesus not personally intervened, they would actually have cast Mary out of their fellowship.

To this day it is all too easy for Christ's modern disciples to fall into the same pattern of condemning model Christian experience. Let there be unusual devotion to Christ, unusual love, unusual contrition, unusual insight, and someone (as did Judas) is sure to raise the cry, "Fanaticism!" It never fails; others nod their heads in agreement, as the modern-day "eleven" mistakenly followed Judas's lead.

"Be not be overly righteous.... Do not be overly wicked" (Ecclesiastes 7:16, 17) has been so quoted out of context and so misunderstood that the world has been encouraged by the church to regard evil not as evil nor good as good, but enthusiastic devotion to either as less preferable than a middle-of-the-road compromise between the two. Alcoholics, scam artists, and prostitutes who go to extremes in evil are roundly condemned, and likewise such devoted ardor as moved the heart of Mary to expression out of the ordinary norm is feared and shunned, and even condemned.

The twelve disciples at Bethany partook of this spirit of worldliness by condemning as fanatical the love which Jesus accepted as the true model for His followers. In this end of time, would it not be the tragedy of all ages if we should fall into the same error of condemning as fanaticism the heart devotion aroused by the appreciative sense of Christ's love poured out at the cross?

The nobility of Mary's sacrifice is model Christian experience.

The "good work" Mary wrought upon the Savior was more than a useful or meritorious deed. The Greek word (*kalos*) translated *good* implies something beautiful and noble, morally exquisite.

What was so noble about Mary's act? *She did it with no thought of securing reward.* She had spent her all to buy the alabaster flask of ointment without the slightest expectation of hearing herself praised or justified by the Savior. No selfish concern for reward clouded the sheer beauty of the flame of her devotion. When love prompted her to action, it transcended both faith and hope and thus proved itself the "greatest of these."

In this respect Mary is the model Christian. Devotion to Christ cannot burn bright and clear when its motivation is either fear of punishment or hope of reward. If we serve Him because of what we want or because we fear punishment, we are ultimately legalists. In fact, to be "under the law" is to be under the compulsion of self-seeking, even when the reward lies beyond this life. "If righteousness comes through the law, then Christ died in vain." Galatians 2:21.

Put into modem words, Paul's conviction is this: if genuine faithfulness and goodness can be induced by concern for reward or fear of punishment, *then the cross of Calvary means nothing.* "I do not frustrate the grace of God," he insists; the cross is everything or it is nothing! Faith is not a fire-escape plan, nor a glorified social security program, appealing to man's innate selfishness of soul.

The principle of the cross does not justify itself as a calculating, clever transaction by which we surrender something of lesser value (such as present happiness) for a future good, a profitable bargain. Salvation is not presented in Scripture as the profit we gain from business trading on faith. Salvation is indeed most certainly profitable, infinitely so, and a tremendous bargain beyond all calculation; but faith, prophesying only "in part," has her eyes closed as she leads to the cross, and only love (*agape*) enables us to see beyond its present darkness.

All of us are tested eventually to determine whether our faith is merely a self-seeking exercise. In the hour of ultimate trial, love alone assumes the leadership, and both faith and hope are subservient. Therefore "the greatest of these is love."

Let grace do its perfect work. Let's get ready for the final test!

MARY'S LOVE WILL FINISH THE GOSPEL TASK IN ALL THE WORLD.

The most serious problem facing the church is the task of proclaiming the gospel in all the world so that everyone is fully aroused to its claims, either to believe intelligently, or to reject it knowingly. This task must be completed before the long-awaited return of Jesus can take place. "This gospel of the kingdom will be preached in all the world as a witness to all the nations, and then the end will come." Matthew 24:14.

Good men have wrestled with this problem for generations. Despite the best efforts of all churches, the task actually becomes greater with each passing generation. At the present rate of progress, souls are being born faster than the combined efforts of all Christian churches to reach the world with an impressive presentation of the gospel.

Understandably, sincere men have sought to discover ways and means of hastening this divinely appointed task. Committees have evolved all kinds of programs and campaigns, including the use of every possible technological invention such as TV, radio, satellite, Internet.

Can Mary's sacrifice point us to the ultimately efficient way? There are several lessons Mary can teach us today:

1. We marvel at the originality of her method. It was utterly unusual. Who would have ever thought to advance the work of the gospel by bringing an "alabaster flask of ointment … very precious" and pouring its contents on Jesus' feet, and then in timid confusion endeavoring to wash His feet with tears and dry them with the best means available, her long, flowing tresses? How thoughtless, not to anticipate the need for a towel!

Her critics would judge that she bungled her performance. No cold-hearted committee ever thought up a method of doing a "good work" such as Mary wrought. We see here the resourceful ingenuity of love. Only such contrite love awakened by repentance can possibly think up the new ways and means that will finish Christ's work on earth. This gospel, of which Jesus spoke when He commended Mary, cannot be preached throughout the whole world without the inventive genius of her love. The frustrating attempts of formalism are the methods of lukewarmness; foolish extremes are the method of self-centered fanaticism; but the efficiency of love is the method of contrition. It will work; and when it begins, the task will soon be finished!

2. We are impressed that Mary's love became prophetic. The disciples had been repeatedly instructed about the Savior's approaching death and burial, but they could not grasp the reality of it. Mary alone was able to sense the significance of what was to happen. With an intuition more deeply penetrating than that of any of the Twelve, she read the future. Taught by the infallible promptings of love, she had come to anoint His body "beforehand … for burial." Alexander Bruce says, "Thus is love prescient. Such as Mary can divine."

In the exercise of her prophetic insight does she represent the church, or only a rare individual in the church? Is it the Lord's will that eventually such insight be imparted to all?

Tucked away in the Old Testament is an inspired prayer that is yet to be answered. Seventy chosen men from the camp of Israel were gathered about the tabernacle to share the prophetic gift bestowed on the overworked Moses. The Lord graciously "took of the Spirit that was upon him, and placed the same upon the seventy elders: and it happened, when the Spirit rested upon them, that they prophesied."

Then something happened that was not anticipated. Two men not gathered with the official group also received the same Spirit, "and they prophesied in the camp." An excited messenger ran to tell Moses and Joshua of this unofficial irregularity. Joshua was disturbed: "Moses, my Lord, forbid them!"

But Moses had a deeper understanding of the scope of the prophetic gift promised to the church: "Are you zealous for my sake? Oh, that *all* the Lord's people were prophets, and that the Lord would put His Spirit upon them!" See Numbers 11:24-29. Joel adds that in the last days the Spirit will be poured out "on *all* flesh." Then will the long-awaited gifts of the Spirit be fully restored in the church.

As surely as day follows night, the experience of Mary's love awakened in the church today will reproduce her prophetic insight as the fruit of love. When perfect love casts out fear, it will also cast out disunity. Partakers of one Spirit, all will know the unfailing "unity of the Spirit in the bond of peace." Ephesians 4:3, 4. All will recognize truth because it is truth, not because an authoritative spokesman has recognized it for them and excused them from the necessity of discernment. Thus Moses' prayer will be granted.

3. The power to love is paralyzed by the drug effects of lukewarmness. Love is a secret chamber of the soul which can be reached only by the gateway of contrition. And that, in turn, can be reached only by the way of the cross, whereon self is crucified with Christ.

In this light, the lukewarmness of Laodicea, is seen to be a refusal, doubtless unconscious, of the principle of the cross.

Love alone being capable of prophetic insight, and love being benumbed by lukewarmness, the gifts of the Spirit must lie latent and dormant until love is awakened. Moses' prayer indicates that it is God's plan to lead His people into "the glorious liberty of the children of God." Romans 8:21. Then will every "Mary" know "beforehand" not to anoint

His body to the burying, as once she knew to do, but to prepare for Him a crown. Love will know just what to do at just the right time.

4. Judas's monetary appraisal of Mary's offering disturbs our conscience. "Why was this fragrant oil wasted? It could have been sold for more than three hundred denarii." Statistics were all that Judas could think about. All too often we are obsessed with them too.

But Mary's love cannot be measured by computers. The attempts to gauge it thus reveal an ignorance of its nature. All our attempts to measure love's devotion by statistical sheets are condemned by the simple story of Bethany. Love brings her offering with tears, not with self-congratulatory per capita sheets.

In the terrific strain of last-day events, the surest way for the church to go out of business is to try to stay in business "as usual," content to measure calculated progress by trivial percentage gains year by year. Our evangelism must be Mary's method of contrite love. God grant the gift! Finally, we discern in the heart-moving story of Mary the answer to a question in the hearts of many.

5. Just what is "righteousness by faith"? "Righteousness" is not a perplexing concept. Although we cannot see Christ in the flesh so as to know what righteousness is, His representative on earth, the Holy Spirit, imparts to the human soul a vivid concept of what it is. "When He [the Holy Spirit] comes, He will convince the world . . . concerning righteousness, because I go to the Father, and you will see Me no more." John 16: 8-10, RSV. Christ likeness of character is the true definition of "righteousness."

But how to attain this ideal of righteousness is the problem. The "how" is declared in Scripture to be the way of faith.

But what is faith?

Multitudinous and perplexing are the answers given to this question. Some say it is one thing; some say it is another. If only the Lord had told us clearly in easily understood terms what faith is! "Wherever this gospel is preached throughout the whole world," Mary's deed of love will illuminate the true meaning of this all-important word, *faith.*

From time to time, Jesus warmly commended the faith of various individuals whom He healed. But His commendation of Mary sets the crowning seal of perfection to His growing definition of "faith."

He had said to the cold-hearted Simon, "Her sins, which are many, are forgiven, for she loved much." Luke 7:47. Clearly, Mary *loved* much because she knew she had been *forgiven* much.

She probably felt, however, as many since have felt, that she yet wanted faith. This simple contrite love she knew—what good would it be if she knew not that greater virtue of faith which alone could get something done, like moving mountains? Yes, Mary knew she was least in the kingdom of God!

Imagine her surprise to hear Jesus assign His own definition to her experience of contrite love, as He told her, "Your *faith* has saved you. Go in peace." Verse 50.

■ Not with the cold intellect, but with the melting heart, "one believes unto righteousness." Romans 10:10.

■ Whatever faith is in its wide embrace of many virtues, including trust, confidence, strength to lay hold of God's promises, courage, reliance, or conviction of truthful doctrines, its common denominator always present is a heartfelt appreciation of the love of Christ seen at Calvary.

■ *Faith is the human response to divine love.* That is the lesson this story has to teach us! What "avails" everything is "faith working through love." Galatians 5:6.

Look to Calvary. Unless you elect to trample the crucified Christ underfoot, unless you join the great rebel in crucifying Him afresh, your honest heart will respond with that same faith. The phenomenon of such a response is as sure as heaven. God has staked the honor and stability of His throne upon its certainty!

Is that response struggling for birth within you?

Yes, without a doubt, for "God has dealt to each one a measure of faith." Romans 12:3. This is the seed which He implants in every human heart, including yours. If you let it take root, if you choose not to dig it up or stamp it out or choke it to death, *it will transform you into the person you long to be.*

Speaking of His cross, Christ says, "I ... will draw *all* peoples to Myself." John 12:32. He actively draws you, takes the initiative repeatedly, persists in spite of your perverseness and your hanging back.

Yield, and you know firsthand what a penitent sinner's faith can be. Its miracle is the pledge that all God's promises are true, that all your dreams are even now being fulfilled; it is "the substance of things hoped for, the evidence of things not seen." Hebrews 11:1.

Yield, and you know for sure that God is real. The cross has revealed Him to you.

> O for a heart to praise my God!
>   A heart from sin set free,
> A heart that always feels Thy blood
>   So freely shed for me.
>
> A heart in every thought renewed,
>   And full of love divine,
> Perfect, and right, and pure, and good,
>   A copy, Lord, of Thine.
>   ⤳ Charles Wesley

Chapter 13

WHAT DID CHRIST ACCOMPLISH ON HIS CROSS?

One More Important Question Remains

⌐∽

I COULD NOT DOUBT THAT THE DEATH OF JESUS ON HIS CROSS WAS REAL.

■ He "poured out His soul unto death," an infinite sacrifice. Isaiah 53:12.

■ He could not have "emptied Himself" more. Like when one turns a glass upside down to drain it to its last drop, He made a commitment to drain Himself of everything dear to Him, even life. Philippians 2:5-8, RSV.

■ He endured the "curse" of God, which is Heaven's total condemnation. Galatians 3:13.

■ This is how He "tasted death [the second] for everyone." Hebrews 2:9.

■ He "*gave* Himself for our sins," holding nothing back. Galatians 1:4.

■ It must be said reverently, softly, in awe: He went to hell in our behalf in order to save us. Psalm 16:10; Acts 2:25-27.

■ So great was His love (*agape*)! 1 John 4:9-14.

121

But the question haunted me for years: *what did He accomplish? Was His sacrifice a real success?* Or did Satan succeed in hampering or partially destroying what He accomplished?

Through the centuries, people wiser than I have wrestled with those questions. But someone helped me find an answer in Romans 5:15-18 that seemed to say that Christ's sacrifice was wonderfully successful:

> "God's act of grace is out of all proportion to Adam's wrongdoing. For if the wrongdoing of that one man brought death upon so many [Greek: the many meaning all], its effect is vastly exceeded by the grace of God and the gift that came to so many by the grace of the one man, Jesus Christ. And again, the gift of God is not to be compared in its effect with that one man's sin; for the judicial action, following on the one offence, resulted in a verdict of condemnation, but the act of grace, following on so many misdeeds, resulted in a verdict of acquittal. … It follows, then, that as the result of one misdeed was condemnation for all people, so the result of one righteous act is acquittal and life for all." Romans 5:15-18, REB.

How could one get better Good News than that? But then, that problem. Not everybody agrees. Some think they see fine print somewhere. I couldn't imagine how God could contradict that, but through the centuries some have tried to explain away what I thought Paul said. There are several attempts:

1. Strict Calvinism.

To put this idea in simple language, Christ did not intend to die for "all people." In fact, some of its prominent spokesmen have said frankly He didn't even love "all people." He loved and died only for a special group known as "the elect."

The idea is that God has predestined some people to be saved; and because this is His "sovereign will," not even they can thwart what He has purposed to do. The predestined ones go to heaven whether they want to or not.

In one sense, that may sound reasonable. Strict Calvinists feel forced to this position because of their view of the irresistible "sovereignty" of God. If He wills something, man cannot counteract His will. They understand the Lord's Prayer to say, "Thy will *must and will* be done in earth as it is in heaven."

THAT'S ONE SIDE OF THE CALVINISM COIN.

The other side has been the "double predestination" idea that God has predetermined that the rest of people must be lost, even if they want to be saved, and may even try hard to be. (I was reared in a church that favored this doctrine.)   It's "good news" if you are one of the lucky ones; but the others? Too bad.

But when I began to read the Bible for myself, I discovered some things that seemed to be very good news:

■ The very last page of the Bible contradicts this distorted view of Jesus; it brought immense joy to my heart: "The Spirit and the Bride say, 'Come!' And let him who hears say, 'Come!' And let him who thirsts come. Whoever desires, let him take the water of life freely." Revelation 22:17. It would be awful if it turned out that I wasn't invited; could that "whoever" include me? Yes, I *am* invited!

■ Jesus promised: "The one who comes to Me I will by no means cast out." John 6:37. "Come to Me, all you who labor and are heavy laden, and I will give you rest. ... My yoke is easy and My burden is light." Matthew 11:28, 30. The more I thought about this, the more I began to believe that the gospel is really very Good News: has God actually chosen *everyone* to be saved, that is, who is willing to "come"?

■ There was Isaiah 45:22: "Look to Me, and be saved, all you ends of the earth!" I would have to get off of the "end of the earth" not to get *that* invitation.

▪ Then I discovered sixteen first person plural pronouns in Isaiah 53:1-6; each "we" and "us" and "our" must mean everybody, because it's the "we all" who have sinned: "Surely He has borne *our* griefs and carried *our* sorrows ... He was wounded for *our* transgressions, He was bruised for *our* iniquities; the chastisement for *our* peace was upon Him, and by His stripes we are healed. *All we* like sheep have gone astray; *we* have turned, every one, to his own way; and the Lord has laid on Him the iniquity of *us* all." The "us all" must include me.

▪ Then there was John 1:29: "Behold! The Lamb of God who takes away the sin of the world!" None of us has come from the planet Mars; it must be that He takes away *my* sin.

▪ And John 4:42 says Christ's true title is "the Savior of the world," not just of some especially fortunate ones. I had to believe that I am part of that "world." Of course, we all have the power of choice and we *can* reject Him, and many do.

▪ And how could I question John 3:16 that says, "God so loved the world," and "whoever believes in Him should not perish but have everlasting life"? But maybe there is some fine print here: what if God has not given some people the ability to "believe"? Then Romans 12:3 cleared up that problem: "God has dealt to each one a measure of faith."

▪ Who then is going to be lost at last? John 3:17-19 answered: "He who does not believe is condemned.... And this is the condemnation, that the light has come into the world, and men loved darkness rather than light." And there is John 5:30: only those who "will not come" can be lost.

▪ What Jesus said about the Lord's Supper impressed me: "My blood ... is shed for *many* for the remission of sins." Matthew 26:28. Who are the "many"? Since everybody has sinned (Romans 3:23) it must mean that Christ shed His blood for the same "everybody." He said, "Everyone who sees the Son and believes in Him may have everlasting life.... The bread that I shall give is My flesh, which I shall give for the life of the world. Unless you eat the flesh of the Son of Man and drink His blood, you have no life in you." John 6:40, 51, 53. What He gives is universal.

Then I read how Paul says that some people who "eat" do so with unbelief, "not discerning the Lord's body." 1 Corinthians 11:29. Apparently he believed that Christ has done something for every human being.

■ Then I found 1 Timothy 4:10: Christ "is the Savior of all men, especially of those who believe." Every person can think of Him as already his Savior! It was beginning to look certain that Christ accomplished something on His cross that applies to "all men," and no one is excepted. It reminded me of a song I have heard:

> And once again the scene was changed, new earth there
>   seemed to be.
> I saw the Holy City beside the tideless sea.
> The light of God was on its streets, its gates were opened wide,
> *And all who would might enter, and no one was denied.*

■ Could "the everlasting gospel" be news as good as that? Evidently, for 2 Timothy 1:10 went further by saying, "Our Savior Jesus Christ ... has abolished death and brought life and immortality to light through the gospel." How could that be, if the cemeteries are full? It must be the second death. Yes, when Christ died, He abolished it because He suffered it. The lake of fire was never intended for humans, but "for the devil and his angels." Matthew 25:41. The humans who wind up there do so only because they have despised the deliverance Christ has already given them, as He says, "All those who hate me love death." Proverbs 8:36.

■ Then I discovered Ephesians chapter 1 that gave me tremendous encouragement:

> The "Father of our Lord Jesus Christ, ... chose us in Him before the foundation of the world, ... having predestined us to adoption as sons by Jesus Christ to Himself, according to the good pleasure of His will, ... in [whom] we have redemption through His blood, the

forgiveness of sins, according to the riches of His grace which He made to abound toward us in all wisdom and prudence." Verses 3-8.

Who is the "us"? When at the Jordan River, the Father threw His arms around His Son Jesus, He embraced the human race too, and adopted us "in Him."

Coming back to that statement in Romans 5:15-18, there is a second explanation of this Good News. It doesn't try to explain it away, but it jumps to a wrong conclusion:

2. Universalism.

This is a reaction against Calvinism, and insists that God will at last take every human being to heaven, and no one will be lost, even the most persistently wicked and rebellious.

But the Bible contradicts this. God *wishes* that everyone could be saved (1 Timothy 2:3, 4), but Paul elsewhere has to tell the sad truth that many will refuse. 2 Thessalonians 1:8, 9; 2:8-10. Therefore, much as we might wish that everyone could be saved at last, the Bible won't let us believe that idea. Revelation speaks of people in "number as the sand of the sea" who will finally perish, not because God has rejected them, but because they would not receive the gift He has given them "in Christ." Revelation 20:8-15.

But there remained another explanation of those Good News texts, one that again presented problems:

3. Arminianism, a highly respected Protestant doctrine.

This belief says that the "all men" Paul speaks of in Romans 5 are only those who believe and obey. It arose as a protest against Calvinism, because the double predestination doctrine seemed to create both arrogance and despair. John Wesley tells of people who were so discouraged thinking they were predestined to be lost that they gave up hope; and others, thinking they were "the elect," wanted to sin *ad infinitum* and still be saved. Arminianism arose in an effort to get the truth back on track again.

God actually wants everyone to be saved. Christ has died for everybody, Arminianism said; everybody *can* be saved. And Christ died in order to make a provision so that everyone *could* be saved, but what He accomplished was only *provisional*. The fine print amounts to a big "if."

Could there be an Achilles heel lurking here in this doctrine? If Christ actually *accomplished* nothing for anyone unless he first takes the initiative to believe and obey, then so far as the lost are concerned, it's the same as if He had not died. They end up themselves paying the debt of their own sins, and they will never agree with the song that says "Jesus Paid It All" for them.

The implication is that when the lost die their second death, they will owe no debt to God. They are even; by dying their own second death, they will have balanced their account. They will have fulfilled the Hindu ideal of ultimate karma—they pay up and never needed a Savior.

Does God want them to think that?

My conscience forced me to ask, Did not Jesus truly "pay it all," for everyone?

Some who accept this respected doctrine recognize that there would be no life on this planet unless Christ had died for us all; so yes, our physical life was secured for us by the sacrifice of Christ; but He also gave the animals the same physical life we have. So actually, Christ accomplished nothing more for the human race than He accomplished for the animals, unless we take that all-important initiative upon ourselves to believe and obey. What He did was only provisional, an IF offer.

True, eternal salvation is an offer; but is it only that?

I WAS DISTURBED.

Doesn't the cross of Christ deserve more honor and glory than that? Isn't it true that all the happiness that humans enjoy on this planet is also the purchase of His sacrifice? Didn't Jesus say, "I have come that they may have life, and that they may have it more abundantly"? John 10:10.

Many who will be lost have "lived luxuriously, … clothed in fine linen, purple, and scarlet, and adorned with gold and precious stones and pearls." Revelation 18:7, 16. For every human being, believer and unbeliever alike, Christ "has borne our griefs and carried our sorrows" so that the "more abundant life" we already enjoy, believers and unbelievers alike, has been bought for us by His blood. For everyone, "the chastisement of our peace was upon Him, and by His stripes we are healed.… The Lord has laid on Him the iniquity of us all." Isaiah 53:4-6. Never has even an unbeliever enjoyed any pleasure in life except that Jesus suffered a corresponding sorrow and chastisement.

Could it be that Christ hasn't actually *given* anything to unbelievers more than He gave the animals? Is the "gift" that Paul speaks of in Romans 5:15, 16 only offered to us? Do we get nothing unless we take the initiative? If a friend offers you a gift but doesn't give it, then he hasn't given anything to you. You have no reason to be grateful. You owe him nothing. Credit card banks deluge you with offers of loans, but they give you no gifts. *It's all merely provisional.*

I BEGAN TO THINK THIS MATTER THROUGH TO ITS LOGICAL CONCLUSION.
According to Arminianism, our receiving what Christ offers us is what makes it *become* a "gift." Otherwise He has done nothing more than make us an offer, a kind intention, and we go away with no sense of real gratitude for a *gift given.* We had a significant part in our own salvation. I began to wonder, Does this have something to do with the lukewarmness that pervades the last-days' church of "Laodicea"?

Arminianism is wonderful in that it was a brave response to Calvinism, but the more I thought about it, the more it seemed to come short of the full sunlit truth that the apostles preached. God *gave* His Son, not merely offered to do so; Christ *died* for us, not just offered to. He actually shed His blood "once for all" to redeem us, not merely offered to; He doesn't have to shed it again constantly in the Roman Catholic mass where each adherent requires a new sacrifice. In the long run, those who enter heaven at last will say, Thanks, Jesus for all that You actually *did* for us; we owe everything to You.

But if Arminianism is right, then those who enter heaven can say, "Thanks Jesus for Your good offer; but You didn't *accomplish* anything for us until we did the right thing first to make it effective. We did our part; that's why we're here." Thought through to its ultimate conclusion, this turns out to be salvation-by-faith-plus-by-works.

Could this confused idea of what happened on the cross of Christ be the deeply rooted reason for the lack of zeal that permeates the church worldwide? This doctrine must exert an unconscious influence.

And further, what about the lost at last who stand before the judgment throne? Are they lost because they weren't smart enough to accept a mere offer, or will they be lost because they willfully rejected a gift that was *given* them?

Lastly, I discovered a fourth alternative that seemed to be pure gospel truth.

4. Christ *did* accomplish something for every person!

The Bible seems to make clear that the lost will at last fully realize that Christ *gave* them the *gift* of justification and salvation "in Him," but they threw it away. He did as much for them as He did for the saved people. Their unbelief caused the loss of their souls, unbelief that was more than merely passive. It was an active refusal to repent and be reconciled to God. The lost not only thoughtlessly "neglected so great a salvation;" the Greek word means "they made light of it," scorned it (Hebrews 2:3; Matthew 22:5). They *wanted* to go on being rebellious.

The problem boils down to one simple question: did Christ actually pay the debt for every human sin?

Scripture spells out an unequivocal yes.

This is not an abstract, academic much-ado-about-nothing issue. The answer gives the key to reaching the Muslim, Hindu, Buddhist, Jewish mind. Yes, all those people in "Babylon" whom the Lord calls, "My people" (Revelation 18:4). *The answer also spells the difference between a church being lukewarm, or on fire for the One who died for us.*

PAUL WASN'T LUKEWARM!

The love (*agape*) of Christ compelled [constraineth, KJV] him. When he said that "One died for all," he reasoned that it had to mean that "all died," so that "those who live" cannot in peace of conscience go on living "for themselves." They are constrained henceforth to "live for Him who for their sake died and was raised to life." 2 Corinthians 5:14, 15. Paul saw something that set him on fire for the Lord until that last hour in the Roman Mamertine prison when he laid his head on the block before the executioner, and died for the One who had died for him. "God forbid that I should glory except in the cross," he had said. No glorying in his own response, or his own faith, or his own obedience. That's why he wrote those words that we already noted:

> "The grace of God and the gift [with it] came to *the* many by the grace of the one man, Jesus Christ [in Greek *the* many means all people].... The judicial action, following on ... so many misdeeds, resulted in a verdict of acquittal.... The result of one righteous act is acquittal and life for all."

All the other major Bible versions agree with the Revised English Bible. They render "judicial verdict of acquittal" as "justification." It's not that Christ's sacrifice *makes* everybody to be righteous, but He *treats* every person as though he were righteous, because God accepted the human race "in Christ." He is already reconciled to *you*; now, says Paul, "We implore *you* on Christ's behalf, [you] be reconciled to God." 2 Corinthians 5:19, 20.

WHAT THIS FOURTH VIEW OF WHAT HAPPENED ON THE CROSS HAS MEANT TO ME.

Confronted with objections from some that Paul didn't mean "all people," only those "all" who first do something right to make it effective, I looked again. Paul was plain: the "all" upon whom comes this glorious "verdict of acquittal" are the same "all" who sinned "in Adam." They "all are justified by God's free grace alone, through His act of liberation in the person of Christ Jesus." Romans 3:23, 24, REB. Seven truths here seemed very clear:

- "All ... *sinned.*" That included me.
- The same "all are *justified.*"
- And they are "justified *freely*" (they pay nothing, they merit nothing).
- It's *by grace* (that means free to all undeserving people, without exception).
- And it's not only by grace, it's by grace "*alone.*"
- The "act of liberation" is for *all,* because
- it's "*in the person of Christ Jesus,*" "*the Savior of the world.*"

There were those who worried that believing this would encourage people to go on sinning. I thought about that. What they didn't understand was that genuine faith "works through *agape.*" One can't believe that on the cross Christ legally justified him by grace, without something happening in his heart. It constrains him to be obedient to all the commandments of God, for "*agape* is the fulfillment of the law." Romans 13:10. When you appreciate that "in Christ" God *treats* you as though you were just, then He can transform you and *make* you just "in Christ." It's called justification *by faith.*

I AM INDEBTED TO SOMEONE ELSE FOR THIS BREAKTHROUGH IN UNDERSTANDING.

I must make plain that I wasn't smart enough to think this through. I wandered in perplexity because of this tension between

Calvinism and Arminianism until a friend shared with me a comment from an author who a century ago recovered the heart-warming truth of what Paul said. This brought it into focus for me:

> "'By the righteousness of One the free gift came upon all men unto justification of life.' [Romans 5:18]. There is no exception here. As the condemnation came upon all, so the justification comes upon all. Christ has tasted death for every man. He has given himself for all. Nay, He has given Himself *to* every man. The free gift has come upon *all*. The fact that it is a free gift is evidence that there is no exception. If it came upon only those who have some special qualification, then it would not be a free gift.
>
> "It is a fact, therefore, plainly stated in the Bible, that the gift of righteousness and life in Christ has come to every man on earth. There is not the slightest reason why every man that has ever lived should not be saved unto eternal life, except that they would not have it. So many spurn the gift offered so freely." (*Waggoner on Romans*, by Ellet J. Waggoner, p. 101, emphasis supplied).
>
> "God has dealt to every man a measure of faith, and to all the same measure, for the measure of grace is the measure of faith, and 'unto every one of us is given grace according to the measure of the gift of Christ.' Eph. 4:7. Christ is given without reserve to every man. Heb. 2:9. Therefore, as the same measure of faith and grace is given to all men, all have an equal opportunity to gain the inheritance." (p. 89).
>
> "Do you ask what then can prevent every man from being saved? The answer is, Nothing, except the fact that all men will not keep the faith. If all would keep all that God gives them, all would be saved." (p. 69).

Such precious insight! But the same author said more:

"'God ... wills that *all* men should be saved, and come to the knowledge of the truth.' 1 Timothy 2:4. And He 'accomplishes all things according to the counsel of His will.' Ephesians 1:11. 'Do you mean to teach universal salvation?' someone may ask. We mean to teach just what the Word of God teaches—that 'the grace of God hath appeared, bringing salvation to all men.' Titus 2:11, RV. God has wrought out salvation for every man *and has given it to him,* but the majority spurn it and throw it away. The judgment will reveal the fact that full salvation was given to every man and that the lost have deliberately thrown away their birthright possession." (Waggoner, *The Glad Tidings, Galatians Made Clear,* pp. 13, 14).

"Someone may lightly say, 'Then we are all right; whatever we do is right, so far as the law [of God] is concerned, since we are redeemed.' It is true that all are redeemed, but not all have *accepted* redemption. Many say of Christ, 'We will not have this Man to reign over us,' and thrust the blessing of God from them. But redemption is for all. *All* have been purchased with the precious blood—the life—of Christ, and *all* may be, if they will, free from sin and death." (p. 61).

ᓱ

Our search for the truth of the cross has brought us to a place where profound gratitude must fill our hearts. No wonder people sing those four grand Hallelujah Choruses in Revelation 19:1-6, each grander than Handel's in his *Messiah,*

> "And I heard, as it were, the voice of a great multitude, as the sound of many waters and as the sound of mighty thunderings, saying, 'Alleluia! For the Lord God Omnipotent reigns!'"

When we begin to realize what Christ *accomplished* on His cross, we can't wait until we join our voices to swell the anthem:

> "Worthy is the Lamb who was slain to receive power and riches and wisdom, and strength and honor and glory and blessing!" Revelation 5:12.

Start singing now; you will be happy forever.

Acknowledgments

The ideas in this book grew out of my little "university" in mud and grass houses during long African evenings alone on safari. In the light of kerosene lamps, often under mosquito nets, I studied the soul-stretching works of my mentors, longing to be able to communicate these concepts so enriching to my own spiritual life in language clear enough for African ears.

The result was a series of studies on the cross, presented to congregations in Uganda and Kenya, based entirely on Scripture. From them this little book eventually emerged.

I owe much to that kind Providence which appointed me those quiet years of tuition in Africa. There I learned to sense a need for a clearer understanding of the cross. This hunger was deepened as I had opportunity to peruse unhurriedly the writings of thoughtful authors of previous generations like Alexander Bruce, George Matheson, C. S. Lewis, Reinhold Niebuhr, A. T. Jones, E. J. Waggoner, and H. Wheeler Robinson. They led me to the Bible, which was all I could use as a teaching aid in East Africa. Intensive conversations with thoughtful African pastors and teachers often helped me put these concepts to the acid test of the African pulpit.

If any idea in my pages should bring enrichment to the heart of a reader, I am sure that somehow its origins go back to others long before me.

⤸ Robert J. Wieland

More From the Author of
In Search of the Cross
Robert J. Wieland

Powerful Good News

This book documents how a paralyzing counterfeit has been injected like a drug into our modern concepts of the simple message that should still be "the power of God to salvation." Spiritual frustration, depression, backsliding—all are seen as a failure to perceive or believe how good the *Good News* is. The Bible-based concepts set forth in this book will stir the reader like a breath of fresh air.

Paperback, 143 pages [00125] .. **$6.95**
AudioBook (four cassettes) read by
author [20202] **$10.00**

The Good News Is Better Than You Think

Through the centuries, accretions of bad news have attached themselves to the gospel like barnacles on a ship. Here is a book that courageously cuts out the bad news that theologians have added to the gospel, and restores the pure New Testament idea of *Good News* that once "turned the world upside down." Excellent book for sharing.

Paperback, 95 pp. [00114] **$6.95**

The Gospel in Revelation:
Unlocking the Last Book of the Bible

A book whose time has come! Most books about Revelation make it hard to understand, as though God is trying to hide something from us. In this easy-to-understand book, the author has used the tried and proven key to unlock Revelation's mysteries—letting the Bible explain itself. Join him in a chapter-by-chapter, verse-by-verse study to rejoice in the *Good News* in Revelation, and fall in love with John's Apocalypse.

Paperback, 198 pp. [00115] **$6.95**

Further Reading for Your Journey
In Search of the Cross

The Glad Tidings: Galatians Made Clear
by E. J. Waggoner

In the late 1930s, the author of *In Search of the Cross* discovered a rare, out-of-print copy of *The Glad Tidings.* Waggoner had caught a vision that the message of salvation only by faith and the reality of the cross Paul had written about was present truth. Since its original publication in 1900, this verse-by-verse study of Galatians has been republished several times in modern editions and has kindled fires of personal revival in Australia, Africa, Europe, and North America.

Paperback, 144 pages [00113] .. **$6.95**

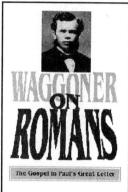